Stories
of
Faith

Stories
of
Faith

by
John Shea

THE THOMAS MORE PRESS
Chicago, Illinois

The author wishes to thank the following for permission to incorporate in his text excerpts from:

Tennessee Williams, *Suddenly Last Summer*. Copyright © 1958 by Tennessee Williams. Reprinted by permission of New Directions.

"Revelation" from *Everything That Rises Must Converge* by Flannery O'Connor. Copyright © 1964, 1965 by the Estate of Mary Flannery O'Connor. Reprinted by permission Farrar, Straus & Giroux, Inc.

The Sword of His Mouth by Robert Tannehill. Copyright © 1975 by The Society of Biblical Literature. Reprinted by permission of Fortress Press.

From *The Awful Rowing Toward God* the poem "Welcome Morning" by Anne Sexton. Copyright © 1975 by Loring Conant, Jr., Executor of the Estate of Anne Sexton. Reprinted by permission of Houghton Mifflin Company.

Cat's Cradle by Kurt Vonnegut Jr. Copyright © 1963 by Kurt Vonnegut Jr. Reprinted by permission of Delacorte Press/Seymour Lawrence.

The New Testament: An Introduction by Norman Perrin. Copyright © 1974 by Norman Perrin. Reprinted by permission of Harcourt Brace Jovanovich, Inc.

Final Payments by Mary Gordon. Copyright © 1978 by Mary Gordon. Reprinted by permission of Random House, Inc.

Pilgrim at Tinker Creek and *Holy the Firm* by Annie Dillard. Copyright © 1974 and 1978 by Annie Dillard. Reprinted by permission of Harper & Row, Inc.

The Odyssey, A Modern Sequel and *Zorba the Greek* by Nikos Kazantzakis. Copyright © 1958 and 1952 by Nikos Kazantzakis. Reprinted by permission of Simon & Schuster, Inc.

The God Who Fell from Heaven by John Shea. Copyright © 1979 by John Shea. Reprinted by permission of Argus Communications.

ISBN 0-88347-112-4

CONTENTS

To the stories
of my
family and friends

Preface

Do not let your hearts be troubled!
Have faith in God
and faith in me.

Gospel of John 14, 1

THIS book is a meditation on the dual drives of Christian faith: toward God and toward Jesus. How do we get to God and, more importantly, how do we get back? How do we contact the vitality of Jesus that generated the Christian movement and what happens to us once contact is made? Faith has the reputation of being a chameleon word. Its meaning changes with the environment. But no matter what transformations occur, God and Jesus are the constant center.

Yet the opening words of the Johannine Christ, "Do not let your hearts be troubled" are themselves troubling. Is faith in Jesus and God such a calming experience? In another Johannine passage, Jesus promises his followers a fate similar to his own. A lynched criminal is certainly a sign of trouble. As for faith in God, it is an equally dangerous endeavor. Divine reality is a dazzling blend of infinite acceptance and infinite demand. Most people who have drunk deeply of God have walked wildly through life. An underlying concern of the following pages is how, in the company of two such trouble producing realities as God and Jesus, our hearts can ever hope to escape turbulence.

This book pursues the themes of its predecessor, *Stories of God*. It relates experiences in story form, views life from an ultimate perspective, wonders how graciousness can be affirmed when it so readily mixes with viciousness, watches the subtle moves of religious language in the formation of personality and community, cherishes the Bible for images more than for thought, and cannot stay away from Jesus no matter how hard it tries. In *Stories of God* the emphasis was on mythic activity—how our stories, in particular the overarching, communally owned stories of the Bible, create worlds. In this book the emphasis is on navigating activity, how our stories help us journey the worlds we have created.

Chapter one begins with what is close at hand. A businessman, a college girl, and a son at the bedside of his dying father are considering their situations in life. There is nothing spectacular about what is happening but they are involved in a revelation-faith process which brings with it an awareness of Mystery. This awareness is a preamble to the question of God which the second chapter explores. Is the Mystery of life ultimately gracious or indifferent toward us? The answer to that question initiates the journey of faith. The journey begins with the faithful presence of the powerful God, a story of undergoing and overcoming. It evolves into the passionate presence of the calling God, a story of the struggle to live out of a gracious God in an ungracious world.

Although storytelling has been present all along, chapter three explicitly considers it. This chapter places our individual lives in the context of the tradition. It observes the rich mix of contemporary and inherited images and stories. It also suggests that the experience of Church occurs when Christians gather and engage in what is basically a storytelling process. The center of the Christian tradition is Jesus and chapter four details the various ways that he is brought along on the journey of faith. The logical procedure of these four chapters is to move first toward God and then toward Jesus. But this is only a general orientation. Jesus and God intermix through all the pages.

Chapters five, six, and seven are not didactic. They do not try to expound the meaning and message of Jesus. They attempt to sing it, off key perhaps, but unabashedly. A Christian culture must always generate secondary forms. The imagination must play with the story of Jesus and resymbolize it under the influences of the present experiences of the Spirit. These chapters attempt to recapture Jesus as an indiscriminate host, a son who must die and a storyteller of God. Of course, in the telling we ourselves are told.

In intention, and I hope in execution, this book is pastoral. In the theological world of today that remark might be more confusing than clarifying. In this context it means the approach to faith in this book comes from the bumps and prods that go on in the homes I party in, the streets I wander through, the classrooms I puzzle in. Although the theological literature has been consulted, this is not an attempt to contribute to the discussion. Academic brillance is often imported because light is a scarce commodity and whatever illumines is welcome. But the audience in mind is not the journal readers. It is ministers, teachers, students, parents, and all who find the question of God unavoidable and the attraction of Jesus irresistible.

Finally, thank yous all around! To my family and friends who with great understanding have put up with the preoccupied stare in my eyes for the last two months. Especially to Rita who typed and retyped.

Chapter One

The Way of Revelation and Faith

We . . . want to be the poets of our lives, and first of all in the smallest and most commonplace matters.[1]
Friedrich Nietzsche

God is the poet of the world, with tender patience leading it by his vision of truth, beauty, and goodness.[2]
Alfred North Whitehead

IT was the late afternoon flight from Cleveland to Chicago. Two men were loudly relaxing over drinks. They were dressed in basic business attire and their scarred attache cases were jammed beneath the seats. The older man was in his late fifties and the younger one around forty. From the conversation a good guess would be that they were the vice-president and sales representative of a small company. They had flown out of Chicago in the morning, made a deal and made it big, and now were on their way back. In the middle of re-hashing their success the older man moved to a new topic.

"This will really make us for the next two years. . . . You know last winter Marge and I went down to see Frank and Janice. You remember Frank? He retired about four years ago. They have a nice home right on the golf course outside of Fort Myers. Two bedrooms, just enough. What they do is fly their grandchildren down one at a time—at school breaks

13

and summers—to get to know them. It hit Marge and me that at our age that's what it is all about."

A college girl has just returned from a lecture by Mother Teresa of Calcutta. She was impressed in spite of the fact that her theology professor had warned her that personal holiness was no substitute for systemic change. She now sits crosslegged on the floor of the living room, tracing lines in the perspiration on a Budweiser can and talking with that bouyant confidence that in the next sentence or two everything will come together. "You know it came to me that people around here are too stuck on themselves. I think that if you went through life and never threw yourself into anything, never found something that you could give yourself to, never got outside yourself, it would be a waste. You have to have a cause. You just can't be doing your own thing."

The eighty-three year old man has been dying for about three weeks. For the last two weeks he has been in the hospital. He is conscious about half the time. His son, Jim, who is around forty-five, comes each day after work and sits by the bedside. He says he wishes his father would open his eyes so they could talk. But the last time the old man was conscious he called his son Joe and asked him if the ice wagon was in the neighborhood. On Friday night just before he left, Jim leaned over to his father. "Oh, Pa, for God's sake let go! Let go! It's got to be better." The old man died early Saturday afternoon. Later,

Jim told the rest of the family he just knew it was the right thing to say.

Although these three mini-stories are about different people in different life settings, a similar human dynamic is going on in each of them. What is happening is the discernment of a truth which seems built into the very grain of the Mystery of life and the enticement to think, feel and act in accord with that truth. This everyday way of proceeding, this ordinary and unavoidable human process goes by the spectacular name of revelation and faith.

Five elements of the revelation-faith process can be discerned in these episodes. (1) There is a relationship to the Mystery of life. (2) This Mystery communicates meanings about the nature of the relationship. (3) This meaning is initially formulated and then pondered, acted on, rephrased, repondered, reacted on, etc. (4) The meaning that is received is related to the conflicts, questions and needs of the people involved. (5) Although there is an enshrined religious vocabulary to talk about the felt perception of these experiences, it is seldom used. This last element is a special characteristic of contemporary relevation-faith experiences.

Before we explore these elements, two considerations should be noted. First, the people involved are not explicitly aware of these elements. They are concerned with the *content* of what is happening. They have life decisions to make and they are about the business of making them. The phrase "revelation-faith" initially points to a *process*, a specific way of knowing, feeling, and consequently

15

acting. It details the structure of certain experiences. It is an x-ray approach which is interested in a picture of the skeletal components.
Therefore, to use these brief incidents to investigate
the ordinary ways of the revelation-faith process
means to take clues from the language and general
attitudes of the people. It is to infer, surmise, and
suggest. It is, in effect, to say: "If you wanted to look
at your experience from a process perspective, this
might be what was happening."

Secondly, these are real people and their life
stories are indisputably their own. Yet what is
present in their experiences are conditions which
prevail in all our lives at one time or another. We
share human life with them and so what comes to
light in their stories can illuminate our own. What
James Olney has said of autobiography is true of any
meeting with another life: "(It) engages our interest
and holds it and that in the end seems to mean the
most to us because it brings an increased awareness,
through an understanding of another life in another
time and place, of the nature of our own selves and
our share in the human condition."[3] This is not a
glorification of self-preoccupation but the simple
recognition that we not only enter into our own lives
directly but also through the life stories of those we
meet.

THE ELEMENTS OF REVELATION—
FAITH EXPERIENCES

1. Certain events of our lives bring with them the
awareness that we have a relationship not only to

the events themselves but also to the Mystery of life within which they occur. In his brief visit with his retired friend the businessman becomes aware of the life process he is participating in. He does not stop at saying, "Frank and Janice have a good thing going." He takes what they are doing as symbolic of a basic life meaning. "That's what it's all about." The college girl's brush with a committed woman triggers in her the awareness that she is related to a larger Mystery. She ponders what would make life worthwhile and what would make it a waste. The dialogue is not between her and Mother Teresa, but between her and the Mystery of life mediated through Mother Teresa. The son at his father's bedside becomes aware that he is living and his father is dying within a larger Mystery which they both share. His language signals this awareness in the common phrase, "For God's sake." In the first moment revelation-faith experiences make us aware of a fact that we often overlook. We come and go within a larger Mystery.

This way of becoming aware of the ultimate Mystery within which "we live and move and have our being" might be characterized as the "in and through" approach. In and through the visit, in and through the lecture, in and through the hospital watch the relationship to ultimate Mystery enters the minds and hearts of the people involved. "In and through" are the favorite prepositions of much of contemporary philosophical theology.

For at least the presence of God as the transcendental ground and horizon of everything which exists and

17

everything which knows (and this is a presence of God, an immediacy to him) takes place precisely *in and through* the presence of the finite existent.[4]

We attain God only *in and through* the intramundane, of whose being he is the fountainhead.[5]

These quotes from Rahner and Schillebeeckx refer to a particular interpretation of the ultimate meaning of the Mystery, namely that it is the loving reality we call God. But for our immediate purposes it is the process of encounter that is important. Life Itself, the Mystery, the Whole, the Encompassing, the More is not a reality we directly encounter. It is always mediated through our interaction with our concrete situations. In Schillebeeckx's suggestive language the Mystery appears as a "transcendent third."[6]

In principle any encounter can bring with it the awareness of a relationship to Life Itself. Since all interaction occurs within the Mystery of human existence, any interaction can be the vehicle of its presence. The oral and written history of contact with Mystery is a chronicle of the unexpected. People have become aware of Mystery in privies and parks, in beds and on mountains, at times of joy and despair, in interaction with both friends and enemies, battling the larger systems of society and searching the depths of the solitary self, gazing at the vastness of the sky and squinting at the intricacies which swarm at the other end of a microscope. There seem to be no rules for the arrival of this awareness. The implications of this fact are many, but one immediately suggests itself. Each person's life story must be told and heard from the perspective of which events brought the awareness of a relationship to Mystery. These stories and the meanings which the person has distilled from them are the starting point for religious development.

Revelation-faith experiences do not bring an awareness of people in themselves or the Mystery in itself. They focus on the relationship between people and the Mystery. What is revealed and responded to is not the fact that there is a Mystery, but the fact that we are bonded to that Mystery. What is revealed and responded to is not the fact that there are "deep parts of us," but the fact that our relationship to Mystery makes us people of depth. Also this relationship is perceived as real or in the current jargon has a "strong accent of reality." The Mystery which we have encountered is truly other than we are. It is not an abstraction of mind, the product of a purely mental act that moves from concrete particulars to the generalized notion of Mystery without any encouragement from the encountered reality. Contact with the Mystery may excite personal or group enthusiasm, but the Mystery cannot be reduced to this enthusiasm. Although this Mystery is genuinely other, it is an otherness which we participate in. The Mystery has all the "recalcitrant feel" of objective reality, but we cannot treat it in a detached way because it is an objective reality which always involves us. Therefore the first element of revelation-faith experiences is that in and through our concrete interactions we are involved in a real relationship with a Mystery.[7]

2. What is recognized in a revelation-faith experience is not just the stark, skeletal structure of a relationship. A meaning about the flow of that relationship is also present. The second element concerns the way this meaning comes about. It appears as given. The businessman did not look at his options and then logically argue that he must be in contact with his grandchildren. It "hit" him. It "jumped out of" his experience, appearing as invitation he had very little to do with. The college girl did not go to the lecture with an upfront agenda, but at the lecture something "came to her." Her simple language reflects the felt perception that the meaning somehow arrived. She received it more than she manufactured it. The son who encourages his father to let go is perhaps the clearest example that the meaning has a given quality about it. His way of justifying to the family what he said could be paraphrased as: "This was the truth about the situation and I responded. I didn't take it on my own but only spoke what was already there." The felt perception that a meaning is communicated from the Mystery rather than fabricated by the person is a sensitive awareness but one that is at the heart of the experience.

In revelation-faith experiences Mystery is sensed as "being on the make." It initiates the relationship. We are in a situation of response. At these times we are not clever detectives finding reluctant clues. The experience is not one of assertive people and receding Mystery. The Mystery is unveiling itself, freely disclosing the quality of our relationship with it. It is this sensitivity—that the Mystery moves toward us—which is the experiential base for all talk of "grace."

The received meaning not only appears as given but also has the quality of an imperative. It "comes on" as an invitation which can be rejected only at possible personal peril. Since the Mystery is greater than any of its inhabitants, its communications to those who are within it are naturally received as commands. The meanings are indications of how life is to be lived if it is to be in sync with the Mystery which is its source and destiny. As such, the meanings do not appear as options but as truths which must be conformed to. When the businessman says, "That's what it is all about," the next sentence, whether spoken or not, is, "That is what I must be about." The college girl formulates the meaning that a self-centered life is a waste. This way of talking does not give the impression that she feels that a self-centered life is a viable choice. She feels a demand from the Mystery to be other-centered. The words the son speaks to his dying father are in some way pulled from him. In order to say, "Let go!" when all his life he had said, "Hang on!" he had to experience the meaning as a powerful force. While the communicated meanings can be resisted, they make powerful claims on the people involved.

An important quality of the moment of disclosure is that "it is hardly discernible at all by itself, for while it may appear to last through an eon of time, it is nevertheless a wisp which can barely be captured."[8] In other words, the communicated meaning is instantly appropriated. The felt perception that the meaning is given and therefore imperative does not mean it appears in awareness or language untouched by the person who receives it. The given never actually appears as given but only as transformed by its reception. There is an intimate and extremely subtle connection between the self-revelation of the Mystery and its self-expression through the formulation of the receiving person. While the otherness of the Mystery and the gift-like quality of its communication must be maintained, it must also be acknowledged that the formulation of this experience is in terms of the human person. And since by the nature of this experience it is deeply involving, there is no easy way to sort out the "bare communication" from its "personal formulation." What we have of the revelation-faith experience is its faith formulation. Part of that formulation is that the meaning has been given and not "conjured up;" but it is the faith-formulation that tells us that. So the second and third elements are tightly interwoven, able to be distinguished but never separated.

3. Any formulation of the meaning which the person feels has been received will only be a partial appropriation of the actual flow of the relationship. The Mystery to which we are related suffuses our lives; and so we are capable of receiving and expressing its intentions. Yet, it is always transcendent to our lives and so every formulation will always be partial. The businessman expresses the meaning in terms of generativity, the college girl in terms of other-centeredness, and the son in terms of surrender. Yet the meanings of generativity, other-centered-ness and surrender do not exhaust the

activity of the relationship. Schillebeeckx calls the Mystery the "Ultimate-Intimate."[9] As intimate, we receive and articulate our relationship to it. As ultimate, the meaning of our relationship eludes full expression.

The partial character of all faith formulations means the process is open-ended and ongoing. The actual experience may be sudden but its appropriation is usually slow. Revelation-faith experiences carry with them a sense of "too much" and "very important." The result is that the events are remembered, rehashed, and slowly, meanings are clarified. The metaphors for this process are: mining the richness, surfacing the depth, unpacking what is compressed. So the businessman is still talking and testing the meaning he found last winter. The college girl is turning over the impact of Mother Teresa, allowing the meaning to "rinse" through her. The son rehearses what he did, partially looking for approval, but mostly seeking a fuller understanding of how he responded. The meaning of revelation-faith events burst slowly like delayed fireworks over the long days and fast years of our lives.

The process of faith-formulation outlasts the experience that gave rise to it. The experience lingers in memory, visited and revisited until all it has to tell has been told. The result is a distilled meaning. This meaning, now detached from life-giving dialogue with the experience, accompanies the person through life. It often takes the form of a proverb, slogan, or one-line truism. The businessman will say at a cocktail party, "You've got to get to know your grandchildren." The college girl will judge future acquaintances in terms of their self-centeredness. The son will say, "When it's your time, it's your time. You have to go with it." While these crystallized life-learnings can be communicated to others, they often appear arbitrary. Finalized faith-formulations make the most sense when they are related to the whole process which preceeded them.

The phrase "faith-formulation" can give the mistaken impression that responses to a revelatory event are primarily intellectual efforts. And in the history of the theology of revelation and faith the cognitive value of these experiences has been heavily stressed. But the revelation-faith experience itself engulfs the whole person. They affect the centered self, addressing the mind, heart and behavior. In a similar way the faith-formulation process is an activity of the whole person, unfolding the convictions, feelings and behaviors which are suggested in the experience. At any given time the mind or the heart or the need to embody the meaning in action will play the dominant role. But all are always present and operative. However, a certain "pride of place" must be given to action. In action the convictions and feelings are mobilized and tested in the real world. It is in living out the project hidden in the revelation-faith experience that we extend and own, deepen and purge that experience. The last moment of the faith-formulation process is the businessman, the college girl, and the son engaged in a new way in an old world.

4. What happens in the revelation-faith experience is closely connected to what is happening in us

before that experience. The needs that are troubling us, the drives that are urging us on, the conflicts we are engaged in shape the content of the revelation. This does not mean that the revelation is caused by the needs, drives, or conflicts, but that they make us receptive, gear us to specific communications. The story is told that Gertrude Stein on her deathbed was asked, "What is the answer?" She replied, "What is the question?" No revelation is received as an answer until a question has been experienced.

Thomas Fawcett's rendition of the dynamics of a revelation-faith experience explicitly points to the condition previous to the experience.

> (i) The presence of an existential need.
> (ii) The moment of disclosure or perception itself.
> (iii) The embodiment of the experience in symbolic form.[10]

In our three episodes the presence of an existential need is not explicitly stated. Yet, the revelation received and articulated seems to corelate well with what we know of the crises and tasks of the life stage of each person. The late middle-age of the businessman is a time of generativity concerns, how to relate to the coming generation and pass on the life learnings. The early adulthood of the college girl is a time when life styles are envisioned. Her revelation-faith experience concerns an indispensible element of that style. It is likely that the son's long hours of bedside watching had been filled with thoughts of his father's death. How would he take it? What could he do to help? The revelation-faith experience showed a way. Without restricting the myriad ways the Mystery may approach us, our life stories provide the areas to which communications may be addressed.

Fawcett's three point scheme also reenforces the close bonding between the moment of disclosure and the symbolic embodiment. These two elements are so closely linked that in the second moment he uses both the word "disclosure" which indicates a movement from the Mystery to the receiving subject and the word "perception" which points to an active grasping by the subject of the meaning of the Mystery. The second moment immediately bridges into the third. "The moment of perception, therefore, cannot really be separated from its symbolic formulation because the subject can never speak of his experience without the use of a symbol."[11] The revelation-faith experience is a unified process with discernible but inseparable elements.

Stressing the existential need that makes possible but does not coerce the revelation-faith experience can give the impression of a "sweetheart contract." While we are pursuing a certain need, the Mystery is pursuing us. While we are puzzling with a certain question, the Mystery is busy with an answer. Personal quest is met by a gift from beyond. Yet the interchanges with Mystery are often anything but smooth. The existential situation is often not one of sincere search but one of distortion which is not recognized. A life has so gone against the grain of the Mystery within which it lives that the revelation-faith experience is the recognition of its wrongheadedness and the possibility of change. Revelation-faith experiences do match existential situations. But the communicated meaning is often not expected and it is greeted by shock and disbelief. In revelation-faith experiences there may be a way of being receptive but there is no way of control.

Flannery O'Connor's short story, *Revelation*, is a tale of an unwanted message. Ruby Turpin is a "respectable, hard-working, church-going woman" and she thanks Jesus that he has made her herself and not "a nigger or white trash or ugly." While she is waiting in a doctor's office, her whole personality is revealed in the small talk that fills the time. Suddenly a deranged girl, who has overheard the conversation, throws a book at her and hits her over the left eye. The girl tells her, "Go back to hell where you came from, you old wart hog." Ruby is stunned that "she had been singled out for the message though there was trash in the room to whom it might justly been applied." Later while Ruby is hosing down the hogs on her farm, she has a revelation. She looks into the heavens and sees:

> a vast, swinging bridge extending upward from the earth through a field of living fire. Upon it a vast hoard of souls were rumbling toward heaven. There were whole companies of white trash clean for the first time in their lives, and bands of black niggers in white robes, and battalions of freaks and lunatics shouting and clapping and leaping like frogs. And bringing up the end of the procession was a tribe of people whom she recognized at once as those who, like herself and Claud, had always had a little of everything and the God-given wit to use it right.[12]

Ruby's revelation speaks to the overriding concern of her life, but what it says is hardly welcome.

Ruby Turpin is a woman concerned with justification, who is in and who is out, who is on top and who is on the bottom; and she is sure of her place in this salvific hierarchy. It is to this existential concern that the double revelation speaks. First the girl attacks her smugness and overturns her self-righteousness. She is not near the top but a wart hog near the bottom. And later she stares into the pig parlor "as through the very heart of mystery" and then receives the second capstone visionary revelation of reversal. Revelation-faith experiences may appear to come out of the blue, but they always have hidden roots in our life story and speak to our conflicts, needs, and drives.

5. The last element of the revelation-faith process focuses on language. Although each of the experiences cited have definite religious shadings, none of the people express or communicate the meanings in enshrined religious words. At least two of them were active church-goers and had been exposed to religious language through education and Sunday sermons. There is an available vocabulary or, more precisely, a code phrase for the type of experience they were relating and considering. In the popular Christian tradition when people perceive a meaning emanating from the very Mystery of life, they have often tagged it the "will of God." Experiences of the will of God are the receptions of particularized meanings and specific commands to particularized situations and specific settings. In the inherited language of the Christian Catholic tradition

the businessman might have said, "I think this is
what God wants of me now." The college girl might
have said, "I think it is important to discern God's
will and follow it." The adult son might have
resorted to a phrase common in hospital rooms, "He
suffered a lot. It's God's will that he go now." But
none of them used that language so dear to the ear of
the minister.

Some theorists of language hold that when a
specific language is abandoned, the concrete experience it expressed is also lost. In this area this
does not seem to be the case. Our relationship with
Mystery is so inescapable and important that it
inevitably finds expression. When our inherited
vocabulary—God, creation, fall, covenant, sin,
grace, heaven, hell—is not used, religious perceptions do not go unexpressed. A more subtle use of
secular language emerges. People say: "That's what
it's all about;" "Without this it wouldn't be worth
living;" "That's damnable;" "A life without love is
tragic;" "It's pathetic the way she is squandering
her youth." These common remarks are the result of
a faith formulation process that seeks to express the
relational flow between the individual self and the
larger Mystery. The way of expression highlights the
fact that religious language is not a specific
language but a specific use of any language. The
religious dynamic of human life is too powerful not to
have a language. If one language is abandoned,
another is quickly pressed into service.

Although revelation-faith experiences will always
find expression, without the inherited language this

expression is severely restricted. Our relationship to Mystery is articulated only in the language of the present age; and if that age is "unmusical" in this important area of life (as ours most certainly is), we are tempted to Bergman's silence. The Christian vocabulary tells a unique and intricate story about our relationship to the Mystery we live within. Without the richness and subtlety of that language we may begin afresh but we also begin impoverished. The fact that many today bypass that inherited language does not mean that it is permanently moribund. Rather it points to the task that is necessary to enliven it and once again make it serve the present and living God.

This dual tendency—the use of secular language to detail our relationship to Mystery and the inability to use the inherited vocabulary creatively—makes for an uneasy situation in the local church. The inherited vocabulary is still around and solemnly used in liturgies, prayer groups, and in the opening invocations that launch discussions on budgets, education, community welfare, etc. in which the language is never again referred to. The actual life of the community, even when its commitments and convictions are on the line, can be handled in secular language. When any God talk does enter the conversation, there is often an embarrassed silence or the look "what has that got to do with this?" or the bewildering feeling Langdon Gilkey wrote about after reading a theological definition of church:

> Such descriptions of the nature of the Church make good theological reading, but one closes the book (especially if

one has to go off to field work among teenagers) wondering what community in what galaxy has just been described.[13]

This language problem reflects a painful dualism—real life and church life, real language and church language. Real life has its own vocabulary which portrays our interactions with our immediate environments but is silent about the deep convictions and values of those interactions. The church vocabulary cannot reach actual life so it panics and constructs an artificial world. The result of any artificial world is always the same—oppression for those who live within it and irrelevance for those outside.

The only way to bridge the chasm between the enshrined language and contemporary experience is to fashion rope ladders. From one side, the human condition must be interpreted in such a way that it calls for religious symbolization. The pretense that we are self-grounded, that we have no links to the larger Mystery or that whatever links exist are inconsequential is more than an oversight. It is a dangerous simplification. From the other side, the enshrined language must be willing to forego its privileged status. The established Christian vocabulary is often treated as a priceless heirloom rather than a tool of interpretation. While this stems from a legitimate desire to respect the tradition, it often results in isolating the language from any life-giving contact with the rough and ready contemporary scene. The vocabulary forgets its birth in the conflicts of human life and is unable to relate to the enduring patterns of human existence which make it meaningful. Instead of illuminating the Mystery it becomes mystification. In Paul Ricoeur's phrase, the language "thickens"[14] and what is needed is a "loosening" treatment which will make it available for people to use in understanding their lives. For human life to be fully appropriated, experience and religious symbols must mutually interact for, as Eugene Gendlin has remarked, "Feeling without symbolization is blind; symbolization without feeling is empty."[15]

The episodes which have guided our reflection and yielded the elements of the revelation-faith process are the stuff of ordinary life. In the popular imagination the words revelation and faith carry the connotation of exemption. They point to miraculous events, usually situated in the past and always the experience of someone else. Faith is believing on the word of another who was there. We live in the wake of revelation but not in the midst of it. But the revelation-faith process is a natural way of knowing. We are the knowers and the object known (if this type of language can even be used in this area) is the otherness which includes us, the Mystery which we dwell within. The knowledge, attitudes, and actions which come about as a result of revelation-faith experiences can be labeled, "life orientations." Revelation-faith experiences do not produce "how to" hints but fundamental perspectives and attitudes.

When people talk about life, not any of the categories or objects within life but life itself, it is a good guess that they are reflecting an experience which has a revelation-faith structure. When the subject of the sentence is "life," the underlying experience has had the impact of revelation and has been appropriated in the subtle and digestive style we call faith. What experience generated Kierkegaard's insight, "Life can only be understood backwards; but it must be lived forwards?" When did O'Henry come to the conclusion that "Life is made up of sobs, sniffles, and smiles, with sniffles predominating?" What was the context of Ogden Nash's quip, "Life is stepping down a step / or sitting in a chair / And it isn't there?" Certain encounters give off meanings that are applicable not only to that individual happening but to the relationship to life itself which permeates every happening. These meanings are often encapsulated in statements which begin, "Life is . . ."

To anchor revelation and faith in the ordinary processes of human perception and feeling is not to deny special revelation-faith experiences. But these experiences are special not because they bypass the boundaries of ordinary experiencing but because within those boundaries they provide a particularly powerful illumination of our relationship to Mystery. It is the content of what is revealed and not the way of revealing that is extraordinary. The businessman, college girl, and son live within communities which acknowledge certain events and the faith meanings derived from those events as especially revelatory of life. These people will bring, implicitly or explicitly, their revelation-faith experiences to the touchstone events and faith of their communities. But it should be noted that they come with a revelation-faith experience to the established revelation-faith experience which the community suggests is the measure of truth and a defense against illusion. In other words, the fact that they participate in a revelation-faith process makes it possible for them to consult the enshrined revelation-faith process. If there is to be a Revelation-Faith Event in capital letters, there must be revelation-faith events in small letters. This was a strong theme in the theology of William Temple. "Unless all things are revelation, nothing can be revelation. Unless the rising of the sun reveals God, the rising of the Son of Man from the dead cannot reveal God."[16]

The ambition in Nietzsche's remark which opens this chapter is to be a poet of the commonplace. We must be sensitive to the depth of the everyday, to the extraordinary that bursts from the mundane, to the marvelous ways of what we take for granted. Our analysis of the ordinary stories of ordinary people has attempted to uncover a revelation-faith movement so intimate to our lives that it is often overlooked. It is through the poetry of these natural rhythms that we touch upon the poetry of God, which the Whiteheadian quote suggests lures us into beauty. Christophe Luthardt has stated this procedure in a different way. "Everything visible conceals an invisible mystery, and the last mystery of all is God."[17] We have detailed how visible encounters carry our minds and hearts to the awareness of a relationship with an invisible Mystery.

The Way of Revelation and Faith

The last Mystery or, more precisely put, the ultimate meaning of our relationship to Mystery is still to be considered. This is the question of God; and it is raised and answered through the structural elements of the revelation-faith process we have explored. The rhythms at work when the question is generativity or other-centeredness or surrender are also at work when the question is God. Only with the question of God there is often a heightened sense of panic and possibility. The stakes are higher.

Chapter Two

The Revelation of God and the Journey of Faith

Faith is not belief in spite of evidence, but life in scorn of consequences.[1]

Kirsopp Lake

THE businessman, college girl, and son of the previous chapter were engaged in specific life problems. The tasks and crises of their particular stage in life were what preoccupied them. The events which became revelatory for them and the life meanings they distilled from those events matched the immediate concerns of their situations. The question of God works on a different level. It moves beyond the proximate issues of each life stage to ask a more fundamental question. What is the *ultimate* intention of the Mystery in relationship to us? What is the meaning of the Mystery taken as a whole? The question of God initially is not concerned with specific communications within the relationship but with the ineradicable nature of the relationship itself. No matter what the message is perceived to be at any given moment, what is being communicated at every moment? Once this question rambles around the mind and agitates the heart, some encounters take on revelatory impact; and we hesitantly begin to form an answer.

A good example of a man haunted by the God

question and the way a revelation-faith experience provided an answer is Sebastian in Tennessee William's *Suddenly Last Summer*. His mother, Mrs. Venable, is talking to a psychologist after Sebastian has mysteriously died.

We saw the Encantadas, but on the Encantadas we saw something Melville *hadn't* written about. We saw the great sea turtles crawl up out of the sea for annual egg-laying. . . . Once a year the female of the sea turtle crawls up out of the equatorial sea onto the blazing sand-beach of a volcanic island to dig a pit in the sand and deposit her eggs there. It's a long and dreadful thing . . . and when it's finished the exhausted female turtle crawls back to the sea half dead. She never sees her offspring but we did. Sebastian knew exactly when the sea turtle eggs would be hatched out and we returned in time for it. . . . The narrow beach, the color of caviar was all in motion! But the sky was in motion too! . . . Full of flesh-eating birds. . . . They were diving down on the hatched sea turtles, turning them over to expose their soft underside, tearing the undersides open and rending and eating their flesh. Sebastian guessed that possibly only a hundreth of one percent of their number would escape to the sea. . . . My son was looking for God. I mean for a clear image of Him. He spent that whole blazing equatorial day in the crow's nest of the schooner watching this thing on the beach of the Encantadas till it was too dark to see it, and when he came down the rigging he said, 'Well, now I've seen Him!' and he meant God. . . . [And] for several days after that he had a fever, he was delirious with it.[2]

Sebastian was looking for God and an answer came his way. If the fever is any indication, he was not happy with the find.

Sebastian's revelation-faith experience suggests a contemporary phrasing for the God question. In the past the question has been framed, "Does a Supreme Being exist?" or, "Why is there something and not nothing?" or, "Is there purpose, order and meaning in the universe?" Each of these phrasings moves us in different directions and so readies us for different revelation-faith experiences. Yet, as diverse as they are, they do have something in common. They are posed objectively and so, at least in formulation, neglect a crucial aspect which Birkin in D. H. Lawrence's *Women in Love* cannot dismiss. When Gerald dies, Birkin reflects on how

> the eternal creative mystery could dispose of man, and replace him with a finer created being. Just as the horse has taken the place of the mastodon. It was very consoling to Birkin to think this. If humanity ran into a cul de sac, and expended itself, the timeless creative mystery would bring forth some other, finer, more wonderful, some new, more lovely race, to carry on the embodiment of creation.[3]

This praise for the Elan Vital does not last long. When he looks at the "mute matter" of Gerald's body, Birkin is overcome by the loss of him "who had died still having the faith to yield to the mystery." Later Ursula asks him, "But need you despair over Gerald?" Birkin does not hesitate for a moment, "Yes."

Both Sebastian's fever and Birkin's despair add a crucial factor to any inquiry after God. If there is a Supreme Being, does he/she care about us? When we have found the reason why there is something and not nothing, will that reason be solicitous of what we hold to be true and beautiful and good? Does the final purpose have our well-being at heart? Is the hidden order of all things ruthless? Is the final meaning played out at the expense of the players? The most fundamental phrasing of the God question is: "Is the Mystery of life ultimately gracious to all that is within it and, in particular, to this two-legged stand-up who is asking the question, or is it indifferent?"

This phrasing has often been accused of being narcissistic. It appears to put the ego at the center, and then asks if all reality is revolving around it. It is a form of salvationism, a rank expression of our panic and need for safety. It keeps us on the level of a child, as close to the insulation of the womb as possible. Although this danger lurks in the phrasing, it distorts its real intention. The phrasing—gracious or indifferent towards us—arises from the inescapable structure of human existence. To participate in the Mystery is to be permeated by it. We cannot ask the question of God neutrally because, quite simply, we are not neutral about the answer. At one moment our lives appear as given from a source beyond ourselves and at the next they appear as threatened from a source beyond ourselves. The flip side of the question of God is the question of our ultimate identity. The choice is between focusing on this intimate link between personal destiny and ultimate meaning and dealing with the fact of "heavy involvement," or ignoring the self's stake in the question of God and striving for a type of objectivity which, in this dimension of life, is unattainable.

But the real refutation of narcissism is the lives of the people who have lived out of the graciousness of ultimate reality. To foreshadow a later discussion—once we are rooted in graciousness, we have the freedom not to be self-preoccupied. With the assurance of a gracious grounding we are capable of moving beyond our fierce, small worlds and spending our energies on projects other than self-defense. This outward risk is the opposite of safety. The paradox of theistic faith, which is exemplified in the life of Jesus, is that living in relationship to a gracious God means living dangerously in an ungracious world. What can be twisted into a question of egocentric safety is really a question of the radical possibility of an other-centered life.

In a workshop on the experience of God a participant responded to the question, "Is the ultimate mystery you live within gracious or indifferent toward you?" with "You would have to be crazy not to go with graciousness."

Belief in God is encouraged by the fact that the alternative appears so undesirable. An ultimately indifferent reality undercuts the meanings and hopes which are the foundations of our most creative attempts at living. God seems to be the assumption behind our basic intuition that life is worth living. George Santayana has remarked: "That life is worth living is the most necessary of assumptions and, were it not assumed, the most impossible of conclusions."[4] Hans Kung puts it another way. Belief in God provides a "primal reason, primal support and primal meaning"[5] for our fundamental trust in reality. Without this belief what appears to us as given—the basic value and actuality of our lives—goes unsubstantiated. There is no "condition for the possibility" of our trust. We build over the abyss and not on bedrock. Although many today take the stand of heroic nihilism and construct private meanings in the winds of ultimate meaninglessness, most people find this intolerable. They argue that the very ferocity of our need for an ultimate graciousness is an indication that the Mystery is truly gracious. The haunting question of God is initiated by his actual presence. John Bowker has wryly put it, "The possibility cannot be excluded that God is the origin of the sense of God."[6]

This way of arguing is legitimate but can easily slip into a modern form of "wagering." Often there is a panicked tone to this approach. "It must be so because otherwise there would be no meaning; and I don't know if I can take that." In this frame of mind the better reasons for theistic faith are engulfed by the need for theistic faith. The will to believe comes strongly into play and the wager is formulated. The evidence for graciousness or indifference is constantly fluctuating and no definitive solution is in sight. But the benefits of graciousness far outweigh the benefits of indifference. So choose graciousness.

Thinking something like this underlies Tom Waltz's return to theistic faith in Peter DeVries' *Let Me Count the Ways*. "Maybe the whole thing is neurotic, maybe true faith. Certainly it is better than nothingness. Oh, give us the hand of God, if only the back of it."[7] Although theistic faith is a free response of the person, it is not as open ended as this rendition suggests. We choose because we are drawn by the truth. Although we can resist, there is a powerful urge to comply. Revelation-faith experiences include free personal decisions but they are more fundamentally a happening of truth.

The question of graciousness or indifference is one of the contemporary forms of the theism-atheism debate. But what must be kept in mind is that this is a debate between equals. Although theism and atheism are diametrically opposed in terms of what they hold, they are both fundamental assumptions derived from revelation-faith experiences. Atheism is not a restrained position within the bounds of reason and theism an extravagant position outside the bounds of reason. Both are examples of religious faith. "Religious" designates our bondedness to what is ultimate. It is the recognition that there is a transcendent ground to our selfhood. Our immediate environments, so influential in determining our identities and the course of our lives, are not the final determinants. We participate in a larger Mystery which is the permeating context of all we are and in relationship to which our destiny is worked out. "Religious" points to the ontological fact of this relationship and to our dim, fleeting, but never quite eliminated awareness of it. "Faith" designates the way that this relationship enters our awareness. We become aware of this relationship because certain events disclose its structure and communicate to us its qualities. Faith is always linked to revelation and is the natural way of encountering Mystery. Therefore, "religious faith" is a neutral phrase referring to the way we come to know the ultimate meaning of our relationship to Mystery.

This is not the conventional use of the term

"religious faith." Usually it is synonymous with theistic religious faith. To have faith is to believe in God. Although this is the accepted way of talking, it has a dangerous underside. It can lead to an elitist position which in the name of protecting faith and making it special ultimately discredits it. This elitist understanding often lurks behind such common phrases as, "In faith we know . . .", or "With the eyes of faith we see . . .", or "Those with the gift of faith . . .". Although this language can be correctly understood, it often has the cumulative effect of dividing the human race between those with faith and those without it. Faith unwittingly becomes a special gift given to a special few. This tendency to talk about believers and unbelievers obscures the fact that all people work out of faith assumptions based on revelatory experiences. The question is not: "Do you have faith?" but "What is your faith?"

Faith has developed, what James Mackey calls, outsider status.[8] It is not really a genuine citizen of the human condition but a supernatural import. It is "something different," foreign to the ordinary ways of reason. Two different stereotypes are often contrasted. The people of faith hold certain convictions based on mystical interludes or supernaturally implanted knowledge or the external authority of sacred writings. They cannot adduce proof for these convictions but they believe them anyway. Why? Because they have faith. The people of reason are a less flighty, more down-to-earth crowd. They are immersed in the rhythms of experience and stick closely to the evidence. They have good reasons for all they hold to be true. When they are faced with insufficient data, they show admirable restraint. What they do not see, they do not believe. The choice this caricature presents is between being a gullible believer or a rational human being.

Pitting faith against reason in this way is a mistaken battle. It does not recognize that all human knowing proceeds from fundamental assumptions which are not argued to but argued from. All efforts of reason are grounded in assumptions derived from revelation-faith experiences; and all faith assumptions are eventually tested in experience and explored by reason. To divide people into the faithful and the reasonable is to miss the fact that faith and reason are complementary processes that are present in every person.

There is a strong tendency to think that if the process of revelation and faith is mystified, it will be safeguarded. If faith is a "secret something" the lucky ones have, the awe, wonder, and mystery of faith will be preserved. But this effort to make faith valuable by making it rare is misguided. Faith is as common and unavoidable as air. The natural process of revelation and faith explored in chapter one is not bypassed when the question is God. Theistic, atheistic, and even agnostic positions are faith assumptions garnered from experiences taken to be revelatory of the ultimate meaning of our relationship to Mystery. To rephrase the emphasis, the specialness of faith is not *that* you have one but *what* one you have.

The question of graciousness or indifference permeates the poetry and prose of Annie Dillard. As a brief aside, it is important to note that theological reflection must heed the poetry, novels, plays, music, film, and painting which attempt to express and communicate the religious sensibilities of the time. "The best textbooks for contemporary natural theologians are not the second-hand theological treatises but the living works of artists who are in touch with the springs of creative imagination."[9] It is the artistic expressions that are the first forms of contemporary revelation-faith experiences. Theological thinking springs from those first products of the imagination's contact with the divine; but it does not, as it has so often been tempted to do, leave those forms behind. To rush past the poetic expression of religious encounters to their derived conceptual formulation is to bypass richness for the sake of clarity. While both image and concept are needed to fully understand any revelation-faith experience, the initial language of the encounter is not "I have five theses to present" but "I saw the Lord seated on a high and lofty throne, with the train of his garment filling the temple."

Annie Dillard begins her Pulitzer-prize-winning *Pilgrim at Tinker Creek* with a story of her old tomcat. In the middle of the night the cat would jump through her window and pounce on her. In the morning she would be covered with pawprints of blood. "I looked as though I'd been painted with roses. . . . What blood was this, and what roses? It could have been the rose of union, the blood of

murder ... ?"[10] This is the question of the basic
ambivalence of life and one which focuses her later
book *Holy the Firm*. What are we to make of a life
which alternately caresses and violates us?

Holy the Firm is the story of three days, November
18th, 19th, and Sunday, the 20th. The first two days
reveal life as capricious, at one moment thrilling us
and at the next terrifying us. The third day, the
Sabbath, is given over to the experience that there is
a reality that holds us beyond thrill and terror.

November 18th is dubbed "new born and salted."
It is a day of wonder and freshness, a day of sky and
mountain and ocean, a day of revelling in the beauty
of Puget Sound (the setting for the days). The god of
this day is a "child, a baby new and filling the
house." November 19th is named "God's tooth." It is
a day of terror and dismay. In a plane crash Julie
Norwich "seven years old burnt her face off." The
God of this day is a glacier. "We live in his shifting
crevices unheard. The god of today is a delinquent, a
barn burner, a punk with a pittance of power in a
match." The contrasts of these gods leads to the
question, to use theological language, of a God
beyond the gods, a Lord of history. In her phrasing
"Is anything firm or is time on the loose?"

Annie Dillard's answer comes on Sunday as she is
walking through the woods. In a knapsack on her
back she is carrying wine to be used at a communion
service. Suddenly she begins to feel the presence of
the wine through the pack and her clothes. She looks
down from her mountain trail into the bay and has a
vision of Christ being baptized. As he rises from the
water, water beads sparkle on his shoulders.

Each one bead is transparent and each has a world. . . . I deepened into a drop and see all that time contains, all the faces and deeps of the worlds and all the earth's contents, every landscape and room, everything living or made or fashioned, all past and future stars, and especially faces, faces like the cells of everything, faces pouring past me talking, and going, and gone. And I am gone.[1]

Out of this mystical revelation-faith experience she proclaims a reality—Holy the Firm. She dedicates herself to this reality as a nun. "Held, held fast by love in the world like the moth in wax, your life a wick, your head on fire with prayer, held utterly outside and in, you sleep alone, if you call that alone, you cry God."

To the question—in the last analysis is our relationship to the transcendent Mystery gracious toward us or indifferent?—comes the revelation-faith experience of Holy the Firm. We are grounded in a reality that cares. But the experience of Sunday, November 20th will pass. Christ will sink back into the bay. Monday the 21st will arrive and perhaps God's tooth will once again gleam. If not on the 21st, then surely someday a disastrous event will threaten our conviction that we are "held, held fast by love." But the Sunday experience is not a repetition of "new born and salted" and so just an "up" day in a life of "up" and "down" days. It is an entirely different caliber of encounter with an entirely different communication. It generates an assurance beyond the capriciousness that continues to characterize human living. As such, it becomes an "anchor," a touchstone experience for the ongoing belief in God.

Annie Dillard is a naturalist and a poet. Her reception of an answer to the question of God has all the trappings of nature mysticism. The lines of Hopkins' famous poem seem an appropriate backdrop:

> The World is charged with the grandeur of God;
> It will flame out, like shining from shook foil.

Yet the intensity of her experience and the magnificent imagery she uses to express and communicate it tend to make her exceptional. For most people the communication of God occurs in and through the more ordinary stuff of life. Interpersonal love, the persistence of hope, the bondedness of people working together for their common well-being, a felt solidarity with people everywhere are some of the experiences people take as clues to the ultimate graciousness of the Mystery.[12]

The jolt into theistic belief, or into the confirmation of theistic belief, through one experience is not the only way the conviction of graciousness arises. People often drift into belief in God out of a number of experiences which have the cumulative effect of revelation. Their faith has an "easiness" and "naturalness" about it. This is not "untroubled theism," the mindless affirmation of love in the face of so much lovelessness. But it is the considered reflection that in the midst of ambiguity the gracious moments are the truth about us and the times of terror a distortion. Of course, absolute intellectual certitude in this area is an illusion. In any conviction of graciousness there is always a leap but it does not have to be the broad jump Kierkegaard envisioned.

Faith in God has many benefits but it does not, as some too quickly claim, make all things un-derstandable. Any answer to the question of ultimate graciousness does not dissolve the question. To say that the last power of human life is love is not to eliminate the question of indifference. In this relationship there is not a once-and-for-all answer which calms us so thoroughly that we can now move on to something else. The experience of a received answer is merely that now there is a perspective, a stance, a posture, an orientation within the con-tinuing ambiguity. The basic conditions which generated the question remain, but we now view them, feel about them and act within them dif-ferently. We may be deeply convinced that poor burnt Julie Norwich and the rest of us dwell in a water bead on the back of Christ, but that will not keep the plane in the air. Before Don Wanderhope in Peter DeVries' *The Blood of the Lamb* falls at the feet of Christ in faith, he throws a cake in the face of a Christ above the entrance of a nearby church. To believe in graciousness is not to live without question.

Not only does the answer of graciousness not remove the question of indifference, but it also generates countless other questions. Once the fundamental contours of the relationship are per-ceived as loving, we feel an obligation to explain and live creatively with all the characteristics of the relationship which appear as indifferent—aging,

illness, death, natural and moral evil. No sooner do
we formulate a faith conviction than we must in-
tegrate into it the chaotic flow of experience. Since
we now have an ultimate perspective, it must shed
light in some way on all that is proximate. We cannot
"cry God" with a self satisfied grin and fall silent.
Hot on the heels of faith comes theology. Theology is
not so much faith seeking understanding as faith
scrambling for respectability in the midst of a
Mystery which it has latched onto firmly enough to
say, "Oh yes!" but not thoroughly enough to say,
"This is how it works."

Revelation is often described as an event which
makes other events intelligible. But since revelation
and faith always go together, a person centered
approach is more accurate. The event does not make
other events intelligible; but we who have received a
meaning through the event try to bring other events
within its sphere of influence without jeopardizing
their integrity. The perennial temptation of this
theological task is to go the way of Procrustes' bed.
Whatever in life does not snugly fit into our thinking
we either stretch or amputate until it does. The
passion is to make things fit at all costs. The classic
instance of this maneuver is the attitude of the
friends of Job. They had decided that suffering is a
punishment for sin, for the all good and powerful
God would not allow the innocent to fall on bad
times. In order to maintain this theological construction of God's justice and power, they must
convict Job of sin. Although Job is adamant that he
has not sinned, they dismiss this as impossible. They

are making the event of Job's suffering intelligible through their theology, but they are doing so at the expense of what is actually happening.

Job's faith seems to fucntion differently. He is able to hang onto the fact of God's graciousness without knowing the ways of that graciousness. This seems to be a characteristic of biblical faith at its best. The three most cited models—Abraham, Job and Jesus—claim that God is faithful to them even in circumstances where evidence of that faithfulness is lacking. Abraham leaves his homeland on God's promise, but "he went out not knowing where he was to go;" Job knows his redeemer lives, but he does not know why he is in such desperate need of redemption or how it will come about; Jesus knows God will not abandon him but he does not know how God will be present to him. This approach of believing in the ultimate graciousness of the relationship but not understanding the ways of graciousness might be characterized as the "despite everything" approach. Hans Kung writes that God is "the mysterious and unshakable ground of what is—despite everything—a meaningful life; the center and depth of man, of human fellowship, of reality as a whole; the final, supreme authority on which everything depends; the Opposite, beyond our control, source of our responsibility."[13] This is an eloquently worded description with the most troubling words sandwiched between the dashes.

The "despite everything" approach is not opposed to faith formulations trying to extend their influence to every sphere of life. In fact, it is passionately committed to that enterprise. But at the same time it is especially sensitive to how tentative and fragile these theological extensions are. On one level this awareness results from the simple fact that theological explanations are often patently un-persuasive. This may simply be the result of Chesterton's observation that we try to get the world into our head when the task is to get our head into the world.

But the deepest source of theological hesitancy comes from the revelation-faith experience itself. What was contacted in the experience is the transcendent side of the immanent Mystery, and the graciousness that was communicated and received is called infinite, eternal, and immense. These words are tip-offs that we acknowledge the relationship as loving but are unable to say much more. Yet the slender fact of love from this source is so over-whelming that we are urged to many words, to many feelings and to many actions. We are always caught between silence in a relationship we cannot fully fathom and unceasing talk in a relationship too powerful to be mute. In this situation we realize that our faith formulations are partial appropriations of unsearchable riches and that theological con-structions are the play of people caught in wonder. This is the basis for the remark that true faith must have moments of anxiety and uncertainty. If it does not, we have settled into a domesticated idea of God rather than allowing ourselves to be swept into the untamed reality of divine transcendence.

Kurt Vonnegut tells a story that is a gloss on the

scriptural one-liner that haunts every affirmation of God. "High as the heavens are above the earth are your ways above ours, O Lord!"

> I once knew an Episcopalian lady in Newport, Rhode Island, who asked me to design and build a doghouse for her great dane. The lady claimed to understand God and His ways of working perfectly. She could not understand why anyone should be puzzled about what had been or about what was going to be.
>
> And yet, when I showed her a blueprint of the doghouse I proposed to build, she said to me, 'I'm sorry, but I never could read one of those things.'
>
> 'Give it to your husband or your minister to pass on to God,' I said, 'and, when God finds a minute, I'm sure he'll explain this doghouse of mine in a way that even you can understand.'
>
> She fired me. I shall never forget her. She believed that God liked people in sailboats much better than He liked people in motorboats. She could not bear to look at a worm. When she saw a worm, she screamed.
>
> She was a fool, and so am I, and so is everyone who thinks he sees what God is doing. [writes Bokonon].[14]

The people who understand this vignette are not the atheists, for all they see is a mock on one particularly naive theist. Nor are they the agnostics, for all they see is a confirmation of the ambiguity they cannot get beyond. It is the believers who understand the story, and through it are returned to the actual relationship to God which by definition does not submit to control but only to adventure.

The "despite everything" approach gives a clue to the concrete way the ultimate graciousness of the

Mystery approaches us. Graciousness certainly does not mean protection from harm. Life is dangerous. Sooner or later it cracks us, and theists and atheists break with equal ease. Neither does the Mystery display its graciousness by providing the inner, ultimate meanings of events, soothing our pain by making it reasonable. Although faith is a continual catalyst which jolts us into ever new patterns of interpretation, it never whispers in our ears that single, clean sentence of explanation which will bring us rest. For every prayer of thanksgiving there is a fist raised toward heaven. Graciousness seems to come down to the fact that we are never alone and that no power which seeks to destroy us has a final claim. This is why in the gospels the sin against the Holy Spirit, the gracious presense of God, is not anger at ourselves for the way we are but despair over the possibility that we can ever be anything else. The true opposite of graciousness is the absence of possibility. To live in the flow of the graciousness that comes from the Mystery is to dwell in the Spirit which St. John calls the companion; and to be with the companion is to venture on the journey.

The Journey of Faith

The journey of faith begins with the conviction of an all powerful and faithful presence. In the struggles of everyday living, belief in God is more a bold statement about overcoming all that oppresses us than an insightful statement about the essential structure of reality. Initially the most significant lines for the journey of faith are from Ps. 139.

> Where can I go from your spirit?
>> from your presence where can I flee?
> If I go up to the heavens, you are there;
>> if I sink to the nether world, you are there.
> If I take the wings of the dawn,
>> if I settle at the farthest limits of the sea,
> Even there your hand shall guide me,
>> and your right hand hold me fast.
> If I say, 'Surely the darkness shall hide me,
>> and the night shall be my light'—
> For you darkness itself is not dark,
>> and night shines as the day.

With the presence of God comes an influx of power. This power is a rock in a weary land and a shoulder of reliance. The ultimate graciousness of our relationship to Mystery is experienced as the power to undergo and overcome, to suffer and to prevail, to struggle and to survive, and, in a perhaps less happy metaphor but one certainly at home in the Christian tradition, to fight and to win.

The central Christian story of Jesus stresses the fact that the graciousness of God means the power to overcome. Jesus' metaphor for being "held, held fast by love" is Abba. His relationship to the Mystery is imaged as generating and forgiving fatherly love. Yet the presence of this love manifests itself as the power of transformation. Throughout the gospel of Mark a holy war rages between Jesus and the powers of destruction. The demons immediately recognize Jesus as the "finger of God" who is able to cast them out. Their power to enslave people is broken by his touch. Mark interprets the mission of Jesus in the story of the strong man. "No one can enter a strong man's house and despoil his property unless he has first put him under restraint. Only then can he plunder his house." Through Jesus, God is plundering the house of Satan. The graciousness of God is a matter of superior strength before it is a matter of superior knowledge.

The resurrection, the capstone of the Christian story, is a symbol of overcoming. It is a direct statement that the relationship between Jesus and God was stronger than the relationship between Jesus and death. The writer of the gospel of John puts this unavoidable meaning into the mouth of Jesus, "I have overcome the world." But this raw fact of victory is quickly put to work as a principle of explanation. This switch is reflected in the phrasing of a question which haunted the early Church and has nagged every subsequent generation of Christians. If God was going to raise Jesus from the dead, why did he have to die? The history of Christianity has never been short on answers to that question; and the answers have never been long on persuasiveness. Even in the story of the road to Emmaus an unprejudiced reader would have to feel the risen Jesus is bullying his fellow travellers into submission rather than answering their question. "What little sense you have! How slow you are to believe all that the prophets have announced! Did not the Messiah have to undergo all this so as to enter into his glory?" The resurrection may proclaim Jesus to be the truth about God but it does not take away the puzzle and pain of his death. The resurrection, at its simplest, is a counter-shock. The shock of Jesus' death is followed by the shock of his resurrection, a surprising piece of love by a surpassing power.

What is not often appreciated is that Christian belief in a continued yet transformed personal existence after death is rooted in the graciousness of our relationship with Mystery. The fact that the Mystery is faithful to us (the symbol of covenant) and that it relates to us as all-powerful love (the symbol of resurreciton) gives us the hope of everlasting life. This hope is symbolized in phrases like "the immortality of the soul" and "the resurrection of the body." Also it is extended into theories of *how* we go on. For example, the soul separates from the body and lives with God. Beyond theories of how we go on, the hope for life after death gives a perspective on life before death. The classic perspective is the reversal of rewards and punishments. In this life the wicked often prosper and the good suffer. In the life to come the just God will rectify this intolerable situation. But the symbols, theories, and perspectives are not the grounding for the belief. They have changed and will continue to change from culture to culture and from age to age. What remains the same is the sense of an inexhaustible, non-abandoning presence. Life after death and the conviction of graciousness are always closely linked because the concerns of power and love merge at this point.

The ways in which presence becomes power are cleverly juxtaposed in the great Old Testament story of Elijah on the lam. Elijah challenged the four hundred and fifty prophets of Baal to a contest to see who worshipped the true God. On Mount Carmel both Elijah and the pagan prophets set up altars on which they laid young bulls, trussed for sacrifice. From morning to noon the prophets of Baal implored their god to come and consume their sacrifice in flame. (As the adage goes, God first cooks what he later eats.) "But there was not a sound; no one answered, and no one was listening." Then Elijah, who had been booing his rivals all morning, poured water over his sacrifice in an added touch of arrogance. He called upon the Lord whose fire came and consumed "the holocaust, wood, stones and dust, and it lapped up the water in the trench." Elijah then seized the losers, dragged them down to the brook Kishon, and slit their throats. All four hundred and fifty.

When Jezebel heard what Elijah had done, she swore an oath to put Elijah's throat in the same condition as those of the prophets of Baal. When Elijah heard what Jezebel had said, he fled into the desert. After one day's journey, he became depressed. He sought shade under a broom tree and prayed for death. "This is enough, O Lord. Take my life, for I am no better than my fathers." (His fathers, of course, are dead.) Out of weariness and despair he falls asleep. As so often happens in biblical stories, an angel arrives, bringing with him a hearth cake and a jug of water. He pokes Elijah awake and tells him to get up and eat. Elijah eats and drinks and falls back to sleep. A second time the angel pokes him. "Get up and eat, else the journey will be too long for you!" He eats and drinks and walks "forty days and forty nights to the mountain of God, Horeb."

The first part of this story is every believer's fantasy. God vindicates his belief in a mighty act of intervention. What else can the response be but immediate conviction ("Seeing this, all the people fell prostrate and said, 'The Lord is God, the Lord is God!' ") and passionate commitment ("Seize the prophets of Baal. Let none of them escape!"). For many this is the *real* way of revelation and faith. Miraculous events elicit tenacious faith, both the faith of the people actually on Mount Carmel on that fateful day of contest and the faith of people today who hear the story. In the last two hundred years both scriptural exegesis and philosophical theology have taken turns in demolishing this approach. There is no need to describe the wreckage they have left; but there is a human flaw in the process that is often overlooked. Paul Claudel has pointed to it in his meditation on Judas. He has Judas say that he would rather watch a cat tightrope along a fence than watch Christ unbend another twisted leg. The response to sudden, overwhelming events is seldom conviction and commitment. The more probable human response is intense curiosity followed, almost inevitably, by boredom. It seems that one of the reasons Jesus refused a request for a sign was that it did not fit in with his mission. The spontaneous reaction to miracle is applause, not personal conversion and renewal.

The second half of the story gives an alternate rendition of power and presence. Under the broom tree it is not a direct intervention of God but an angelophany, which by definition is a less intense experience. If we take the angel as the linguistic symbol that indicates the presence of God and understand the text within the revelation-faith processes we have explored, a meaning of graciousness is focused. Elijah is about to give up: the touch of God is the power to go on.

The graciousness that characterizes our relationship to Mystery is made concrete in the sustenance and encouragement to continue. The extended insight of the story is that in every situation of life the nurture and lure of God is present. This is one of the meanings the Christian cross conveys. To look at a broken man on a cross and say "Son of God" is to say there is no situation where the divine power to undergo and overcome is not present. If this man who is abandoned by friends, church, and state is the presence of God, then no one will be abandoned by that presence. Graciousness is experienced as water and cake in the desert and the unrelenting commands, "Get up!" "Eat!" "Walk!"

God's sustaining and inspiring presence means that we undertake the journey with courage, humility, and humor. Paul Tillich places courage at the heart of faith: "Doubt is not overcome by repression but by courage. Courage does not deny that there is doubt, but it takes the doubt into itself as an expression of its own finitude and affirms the contents of an ultimate concern."[15] In our context the doubt that courage swallows is not the lack of intellectual certitude but the feeling of abandonment. The doubt is "My God, my God, why have you forsaken me?"

An old lady near to death sat still in the rocking chair of the nursing home. "You know I believe, always have, and lived a good life. But now the time is getting close and sometimes I get to wondering." Getting to wondering is the human way. Getting to wondering and moving on is the courage of faith.

This type of courage is reinforced by Miguel de Unamuno's image of the flying spiders who "take flight in the free breezes of the air and even in the midst of a violent storm. . . . These spiders spin those floating threads out of their own entrails, delicate webs by means of which they hurl themselves into space unknown. What an awesome symbol of faith!"[16] Theistic faith risks the unknown. It has the nerve not to shrink from new possibilities and the desire to go beyond the familiar and the comfortable. The courageous aspect of faith bears up under the harmonies and disharmonies of life and finds a creative and liveable synthesis. At the center of any courageous life style is the temptation to boast. But what enables courage to remain courage over the long haul is humility.

Central to understanding humility is the distinction between the essential Mystery and accidental mysteries. Essential Mystery is our relationship to transcendent reality which the more we know about it, the more mind boggling it is. More knowledge means more mystery. Accidental mysteries concern our relationship to all other things and the more we know about them, the less mind boggling they become. More knowledge means less unknown. Humility embraces the limits of the essential mystery while it struggles to move beyond the limits of accidental mysteries.

Humility is not a put-down of the human person but a proper placing, an act of truth not an obsequious gesture. Humble people delight in the power which pulses through them and which they channel; but they never regret that they are not all power. They delight in the love that pulses through them and which they reflect; but they never regret they are not all love. Humility has the same prejudices as comedy and so cannot abide "the man who will not consent to be simply a man, who cannot tolerate himself as an incomplete and conditioned creature, of a particular time and particular space."[17] That is why over the long haul humility remains humility only through humor.

Laughter brings us crashingly back to creaturehood. Just when we have conquered doubt Woody Allen confides to us:

> I am plagued by doubts. What if everything is an illusion and nothing exists? In that case I definitely overpaid for the carpet. If only God would give me some clear sign; like making a large deposit in my name at a Swiss bank.[18]

And just when we have switched to "life without God," bravely staring into the void and mustering as much macho as possible, we read of Stan Waltz who was wakened in the middle of the night by the thunderous explosion of a fireworks factory.[19] His fundamentalist wife persuades him it is the end of the world. Stan quickly repairs to the kitchen where he baptizes himself with water from the tap. And just when we have figured it all out, we hear the mock of all Hassidic tales.

> The great rabbi was dying and, as we all know, deathbed wisdom is the best. So his students lined up, single file, to receive his last words. The most brilliant student was at bedside, the second most brilliant immediately behind him, and so on till the line ended at a pleasant enough fellow who was a good room and a half away. The most brilliant student leaned over to the slowly slipping Rabbi and asked, "Rabbi, what is the meaning of life?" The rabbi groaned, "Life is a river." The most brilliant student turned to the second most brilliant student. "The rabbi said, 'Life is a river.'" And the word was whispered from student to student till it arrived at the pleasant enough fellow who was biting his nails a room and a half away. "What does the Rabbi mean, 'Life is a river?'" he said. And the word was passed back up the line till the most brilliant student leaned once again over the slowly slipping rabbi. "Rabbi, what do you mean, 'Life is a river?'" The rabbi shrugged, "So maybe it's not a river."

Humor reestablishes our awareness of the transcendence of God which we have the tendency every hour of every day to forget.

The journey of faith is walking through life with courage, humility, and humor in the company of God. But this metaphor of companionship can go woefully wrong. It often leads to a saccharine, "me and my best friend" approach to divine reality. God becomes a chameleon. For the radically insecure, he becomes a crutch; for the envious, he is a weapon; for the shrewd, just another angle. This God is a human shadow and must give way to another type of companion hinted at in a beautiful passage from Nikos Kazantzakis' *The Odyssey, A Modern Sequel.*

What is this life, what secret yearning governs it?
There was a time I called its lavish longing God,
and talked and laughed and wept and battled by his side
and thought that he, too, laughed and wept and strove beside me,
but now I suddenly feel I've talked to my own shadow!
God is a labyrinthine quest deep in our heads;
weak slaves think he's the isle of freedom, and moor close,
all the incompetent cross their oars, then cross their hands,
laugh wearily and say, 'The Quest does not exist!'
But I know better in my heart, and rig my sails;
God is wide waterways that branch throughout man's heart.[20]

Without subscribing to any collapse of divine transcendence which might be suggested by this passage, the transformation of God from comrade to quest is significant. It allows divine reality to be itself. The name of God in the book of Exodus can be translated in many ways. One of the most provocative is: "I will be with you as who I am will I be with you." The double fact of presence stated at the beginning and the end, is linked by the sovereign sense of identity, "as who I am." The journey of faith is not any old life with God along for the ride; but a life impelled by the perspectives and values of the divine companion. To journey with God is to walk with him as who he is and not as who we want him to be. There is a twist in the metaphor of journey. We remain the travellers. But God is now more than a companion. He is the path.

The Revelation of God and the Journey of Faith

To live out of the living God and not only out of our own resources and powers is an ancient religious passion. To move in harmony with what is ultimately the case, to ride the rhythms of God is the essence of salvation. The prayer of this passionate desire is: "Breathe in me, O Breath of God." Joseph Bettis has stated it succinctly. "Whereas the purpose of man in relationship to the profane world is to shape it according to his needs, his purpose in relation to the sacred world is to bring himself into conformity with it."[21] Therefore, if the Mystery is truly indifferent, the religious response is to try to live out of that indifference. It does not attempt to twist the Mystery to graciousness for possible personal benefits. Or if the relationship is truly gracious, the effort is to move with the graciousness, even though there may be a personal preference for indifference. Religious passion is initially blind. It does not specify its content. It is a raw drive to think, feel and act out of whatever is the ultimate truth.

This passion—to be one with ultimate reality no matter what its nature—is the motivating force of all truly religious people. Jesus' devastatingly simple reply to the question of why enemies should be loved is: "My Father makes the rain to fall on the wicked and good, the sun to shine on the just and the unjust." The equality of rain and sun could be taken as a sign of cosmic indifference, but Jesus sees it as a sign of universal love. So he places his own efforts at love within that larger Love. Loving enemies may produce more friends or it may lessen the possibilities of war or it may bring about a more just society. If it does, these are taken as signs that love works. Religious people are concerned about the effects of love, but that is not the source of their motivation. In the first moment love is not a strategy for a better society but a command from the heart of reality. "Be perfect as your heavenly Father is perfect" is not a plea to become God but to live in communion with God. In the movie *Manhattan* a friend turns accusingly to Woody Allen and says: "You think you're God." Allen replies: "I have to model myself after someone." We laugh once because we know how ridiculous that remark is. We laughed twice because we know the passion behind that remark.

Nikos Kazantzakis was a man of religious passion. Although he did not believe that the individual's relationship to ultimate reality was gracious, he struggled to place himself totally at the service of what he perceived to be true. He imaged ultimate reality as a great combatant: "I have struggled . . . not to do anything which might find itself in disharmony with the rhythm of the great combatant . . . I work and think now with certainty for I know that my contribution because it follows the profound depths of the universe will not go lost."[22] In *Zorba the Greek* this religious insight is placed in story form.

> I was at an exhibition of Rodin's works, and I had stopped to look at an enormous bronze hand, 'The Hand of God.' This hand was half closed, and in the palm an ecstatic man and woman were embracing and struggling.
>
> A girl came up and stopped beside me. She also looked and was moved at the disquieting, eternal embrace of man and woman. She was slim, well-dressed; and had a

wealth of fair hair, a powerful chin and thin lips. There was something determined and virile about her. I normally hate inviting a conversation, and I do not know what urged me to turn to her and ask:

'What are you thinking about?'

'If only we could escape!' she murmured resentfully.

'And go where? The hand of God is everywhere. There is no salvation. Are you sorry?'

'No. Love may be the most intense joy on earth. It may be. But, now I see that bronze hand, I want to escape.'

'You prefer freedom.'

'Yes.'

'But, supposing it's only when we obey that bronze hand we are free? Supposing the word 'God' didn't have that convenient meaning the masses give it?'[23]

Religious passion wants to "obey the bronze hand." It does not seek to escape but to merge, to be in communion with Ultimate Truth.

The passion to live out of God, to allow him to become the path we walk, means his presence becomes a seductive lure. It encourages in us a complex and dangerous act.[24] This act determines how we will inhabit our relationship to the ultimate graciousness of the Mystery. On our part it entails handing life over to God and receiving it back. On the part of divine reality it entails receiving our life and returning it. This act has an "inner" quality about it. It is an intentional act which we perform out of a spiritual center. We say, "I hand myself over to you, God, and I receive my life back from you as a gift." Although this act can be mapped psychologically, it cannot be reduced to the mental moves that constitute it. We are related to a real Otherness and real transactions go on between ourselves and that reality. Of course, this act must be investigated in the light of all we know about the mechanisms of illusion. But more than psychic tricks are at work. We are initiating the religious process of losing life in order to gain it.

What is handed over to God is everything. Nothing is held back. What we usually resist handing over to God are our extremes, the self at its most noble and the self at its most mean. We tenaciously cling to the achievements and qualities we think make us somebody. We fear that if we let them go, we will be defenseless, having nothing to show for ourselves. We will be indistinguishable from everyone else, sporting only the unimpressive fact of our creation. This seriously jeopardizes our self worth, for we only know ourselves as worthy when we can point to others who are not. If we do not easily let go of our greatness, neither do we readily hand over our smallness. The reason, however, is much different. To hand over to God the meanness of our minds, hearts, and activity is to admit them as ours. Yet we resist acknowledging that ambitions so base, envies so paltry, fears so debilitating, and desires so aberrant could be ours. Letting go of both nobility and meanness means that the total self is involved in the transaction. Divine reality will settle for no less for we live in relationship with a God who, as the prophets insisted, wants broken hearts and not burnt offerings; who sees every giving of "things" as a symbol of the giving of the self; and who is not satisfied by the stall, "Take this! Take that! But do not take me!"

What God hands back is everything. Nothing is

kept. Our nobility and meanness and everything in-between is returned. The result of the handing over and receiving back is, in the language of the tradition, the advent of the new person. We now possess ourselves in and through God's possession of us. Our nobility is a matter for rejoicing but not, as Paul says, a matter of boasting. The greatness we are and the great things we do are initially gifts from beyond ourselves to which we respond. We are not the source but the sacraments of love. Our meanness is accepted and so, in the deepest of all religious paradoxes, transcended. This does not mean that it disappears but that its destructive hold on us is broken. We experience ourselves through a distinction which is perhaps Christian theology's greatest contribution to human wisdom. We love our finitude and battle our sin. The outcome of this process is a tremendous release of energy which goes under the name of freedom. From a religious perspective, radical freedom is not the assertion of the self against all that oppresses it but the ex-perience of the self as funded from beyond. The war cry is not, "We can do anything!" but "In God all things are possible!"

The most significant fact about the returned self is that it bears the marks of the sender. We now carry the agenda of the One who so magnanimously received us and so overwhelmingly gave us back. Our lives are focused by God's concerns. When Christians want to see this new self in action, they look to Jesus. At the time of Jesus it was unthinkable to eat with the crowd of people known generically as "tax collectors and sinners." Jesus ate and drank and rejoiced with them. Why? At the time of Jesus it was unthinkable to engage in any task on the Sabbath. Jesus turned the Sabbath into a day for unravelling withered arms and picking forbidden corn. Why? At the time of Jesus authority was closely guarded, hoarded by those who possessed it. Jesus freely gave his authority to his disciples. Why? At the time of Jesus the roles of master and servant were clearly prescribed. Jesus reversed them, a master's hands at work on the dusty feet of his servants. Why? Jesus does not allow the environment to totally determine his behavior. He acts out of the power and perspective of the One whom he handed himself over to as a carpenter and received himself back as the Son. Jesus carries the cause of God.

The journey of faith becomes awesome when we realize that we travel with the concerns of God. This fact reverses the popular rendition of the God-Person relationship and prompts the street question, "Hey, who's using who?" Our faith in God becomes God's faith in us. Our handing of life over to God is reciprocated by God handing his life over to us. In standard Christian theology, God is the savior of the human race. Kazantzakis calls the human race the saviors of God. God is more than a faithful and powerful presence. He is a presence that provokes. What he provokes is our activity on behalf of his cause. This would be reprehensible manipulation except for the fact that his cause is us.

Jesus' parables of the unjust judge and the hungry friend at midnight suggests two unsuspected characteristics of the divine companion. The common interpretation of these stories is that they are examples of perseverance in prayer. The judge does not give the widow her due at first, but because she is relentless in her request, he gives in. The friend does not gain entry into the house at first, but because he will not stop knocking, the householder finally opens the door and gives him the food he wishes. The point seems to be persistence. God is somewhat like an unjust judge and sleepy householder, but our never-ceasing prayers will eventually turn him just and welcoming.

An alternate interpretation, leaning heavily on the prophetic tradition, identifies the cause of God with the widow and the friend outside and ourselves with the unjust judge and reluctant homeowner. This interpretation reverses our understanding of prayer. Prayer is not the verbal entreaty of a reluctant God but the way we relate and respond to a pursuing God. God is the widow; and if we will not give justice for the sake of justice, she will nag us till we give it out of embarrassment. God is the friend outside; and if we will not give bread out of friendship, he will knock till we give it out of annoyance. God is a knocking and nagging presence pulling us along the path of his justice and love.

There is one certainty about this journey. No one has the same faith formulations at the end as they had at the beginning. The only faith (the guiding insights, feelings, and behaviors) that remains the same is one that remains a clear, clean concept in the ice of the mind or a warm, vanilla feeling in the middle of the chest. If faith propells us into the "thick of things" with the agenda of graciousness, we meet the resistance of the world and ourselves. This resistence forces us to rethink and replan. When it becomes too great, we are tempted to withdraw. But we also encounter possibilities we did not envision, allies we did not suspect. What seemed a dead end becomes the road taken; what was not dared hoped for is suddenly within reach. The expected and the unexpected give faith a history. It develops as we do. The journey of faith turns to adventure when we travel with God as companion and path.

Ian Ramsey describes the cognitive aspect of journeying as a move from a preliminary to a continuing "empirical fit." A preliminary empirical fit means our faith understanding "fits" the circumstances of life well enough to be initially employed as an interpretation. But this opening estimate does not end the process. The faith insight continues to be measured against other experiences and other insights to see if it can withstand the test of both time and life. This is the idea of a continuing empirical fit. Ramsey uses the homely analogy of shopping for shoes to illustrate this process.

> . . . We have a particular doctrine which, like a preferred and selected shoe, starts by appearing to meet our empirical needs. But on closer fitting to the phenomena the shoe may pinch. When tested against future slush or rain it may be proven to be not altogether watertight or it may be comfortable—yet it must not be too comfortable. In this way the test of a shoe is measured by its overall success in meeting a wide range of phenomena, by its overall success in meeting a variety of needs.[25]

This analysis is helpful for it keeps faith in the context of people who have a particular history and whose faith understandings change under the pressures of concrete living.

Yet the movement from preliminary to continuing empirical fit can give the impression of a scientific exercise. Belief means testing a hypothesis and believers sit back and keep score. This misses the key point that faith does not merely encounter difficulties, it creates them. Since faith throws us into life with a mission, we are not in the position of adapting to what happens. We make things happen. Faith precipitates conflicts. The journey of faith is how we incorporate those conflicts into our lives. To live out of an ultimate graciousness in a world that is not gracious is to experience that world as struggle. Initially faith names the fight, and its history is an account of battle. Theistic faith, as so many mystics have seen, is a roundabout way of naming the devil. It is too bland to say the journey of faith is what happens on the road of life. The journey has its own dynamic, creating and incorporating the conflicts which the presence of God inevitably provokes.

Jon Sobrino's sketch of the historical Jesus charts his journey of faith. For Sobrino, Jesus's initial faith undergoes a radical change in the course of his ministry. In the beginning Jesus has absolute confidence in the Father and believes the Kingdom is soon to arrive. To meet the coming God the structures of sin must be denounced and people must be reconciled to one another. The attempt to translate this faith into concrete personal and social forms meets with massive resistance. The crowds no longer follow him, the religious leaders turn hostile, and even his disciples do not understand.

73

This is tagged the "Galilean crisis." The inner change in Jesus' faith is symbolized by geographical moves. He abandons Galilee, heading first for Caesarea Philippi, then on to the District of the Ten Cities, and finally Jerusalem. The conflicts of living out of the gracious God have forced Jesus to reappraise his faith. He still trusts in the Father, but now "that confidence finds nothing in which to root. . . . Letting God remain God now lacks any verification."[26] He still believes in the Kingdom but not in its imminent arrival; and the power of the Kingdom is no longer embodied in miracles but in suffering love. Finally, the sin which earlier had to be denounced and overcome now has to be shouldered. The cross and not the prophetic word and gesture is the way of faith. In Jesus' journey, as mapped by Sobrino, there is both continuity and discontinuity; and the catalyst of change is the actual conflicts caused by the effort to embody his initial faith in the loving God and his Kingdom. Sobrino's analysis focuses on

> . . . the conflict ridden nature of Jesus' faith on the basis of real life experience of conflict, regarding this as a fundamental datum of historical experience. The victory of faith is not given for good once and for all, nor is it a question of 'persevering in the faith.' Instead it is a matter of recovering faith in the presence of something that calls it into deep question: i.e., a pervasive situation of sinfulness.[27]

If the history of Jesus is any indication of the way of faith, then it is a journey of conflict and claim, mission and suffering, a struggle to walk in the ways of graciousness in an ungracious world.

Revelatory experiences disclose to us that in the final analysis our relationship to Mystery is gracious. Despite everything, we know and feel that we are "held, held fast by love." We cry God. But our lives are no safer for it. Nor are we now "in the know." Although we interpret every aspect of life from the conviction of ultimate love, no explanation of all the non-love is forthcoming. All we have is the faithful presence of the powerful God. His energy suffuses us, enabling us to undergo and overcome all that life brings. Bonded to God beyond all breaking we become people of courage, humility, and humor. But to have this God as companion on the journey means we must also take him as path. Our passion is to move with God and he wants us to walk the road which he is hacking out of the wilderness. Our faith is not the still point of the turning world but a force which makes the world turn faster. Our journey is not the way of adjustment in order to survive but the way of struggle in order to transform.

The conclusion seems inescapable. Belief in an ultimate graciousness means proximate trouble. Our only solace is that it is the right kind of trouble; and our only suspicion is that Kierkegaard underestimated when he said faith was swimming in water 70,000 fathoms deep.

Chapter Three

The Event of Church and the Stories of Faith

Old people at evening sitting in the doorways
See in a broken window of the slum
The Burning Bush reflected, and the crumb
For the starving bird is part of the broken Body
Of Christ Who forgives us[1]

Edith Sitwell

PERHAPS we have started in the wrong place.

The businessman, the college girl and the son did not drop from the sky. They grew up within families, ethnic groups, and church communities. The values of generativity, dedication and dying well are not their personal discoveries. People follow the lines set by the larger community more than they set off on their own. If we look beyond the individual episodes, we would see these people taking a clue from the shared values of the groups to which they belong.

Also the question of God and the journey of faith are not new preoccupations of the human race. For Annie Dillard it was Christ, not Buddha or Mohammed, who rose out of the waters of Puget Sound with the world on his back. She belongs to a culture and a tradition which was actively at work in her experience. It seems we cannot talk about our own revelation-faith experiences of ultimate graciousness without resorting to the experiences recorded in our sacred writings. We have the question of God because we have lived in communities with a tradition of telling the stories of God. The language of those stories is available to us as we begin to talk; and we borrow the images and ideas which illumine our lives. Community and tradition are the permeating context of every experience and every interpretation.

Although there is always a dynamic interaction between the individual and the tradition, it seems appropriate to begin with personal experience. Many adult Catholics grew up in a local church that could be characterized as a comprehensive community. Every aspect of life—from everyday meals to special day celebrations—was imbued with either direct or derived religious significance. Tight-knit communities with shared convictions, values and behaviors are a cocoon for the individual. Beliefs are taken for granted rather than personally owned. Today this comprehensive environment of the local church is breaking down.[2] Contemporary Catholics live in many diverse communities. Even within their local church there are pluralistic approaches to religion and life. With the disappearance of monolithic reenforcements for convictions the inherited beliefs naturally come under personal scrutiny. The stated convictions and values of the group are not necessarily shared by every individual within it. In this atmosphere personal experiences and stories should be heard before the traditional experiences and stories are consulted.

Gordon Allport's durable distinction between intrinsic and extrinsic religion is helpful in analyzing this situation. Extrinsic religion is beliefs, values and behaviors which have been received from the larger community but have no roots in the individual's personality. There has been no integration of the basic faith convictions into the life-style of the person. Intrinsic religion is a personal appropriation of the convictions that have been passed on from generation to generation. They actually organize the person's feelings and behaviors. For our purposes this distinction is not between two types of people but a tension that exists in all of us. Of course, no one person can appropriate the entire heritage of the community to which he or she belongs. But the process of critically making our own the faith that has sustained and directed our ancestors is one of the tasks of religious maturity.

T. S. Elliot has remarked: "The tradition cannot be inherited, and if you want it, you must obtain it by great labor."[3] The labor necessary to appropriate the wealth of the tradition must begin by appreciating the basic human condition which the tradition addresses. Unless we are aware of our relationship to the transcendent-immanent Mystery (Chapter One) and haunted by whether that relationship is creative of our well-being or indifferent to our destinies (Chapter Two), we can hardly be interested in an inherited faith which grapples with that relationship. The tradition and the individual must be united by a third experience they both share. If they do not participate in a common human predicament, they have nothing to talk about. The tradition as tradition cannot introduce the individual to God. The reality of God must be experienced and then the tradition, the ageless wisdom about God, can elaborate the nuances of that relationship. There must be an ear that can hear before Scripture can become the Word of God.

Although it is necessary to start with the twists and turns of our own individual lives, we cannot stop there. On the journey of faith we do not travel alone. We walk with others who are our contemporaries. We also remember the journeys of those who came before us; and so we travel with tradition as a guide. Without denying all the other things church is, let us say it begins with people sharing their revelations of God and their journeys of faith. Without denying all the other things tradition is, let us say it is the record of other people's revelations of God and their journeys of faith. Finally, let us put both of these together and say we are a group who is exploring our religious identity by dialoging with the Christian tradition. When we are doing this, we are engaged in the event of Church.

Today many people want to do more than belong to a church. They want to experience church. This is not a rejection of the church in its institutionalized form, a stable community which provides services for its members. But it points to an increased awareness that the Church, besides being a social fact, can be a personal happening. One experience of Christian church occurs when and where people relate to the movement of God in their lives through the understandings of that movement recorded in the tradition. In this context the word tradition takes in everything. Tradition includes the Bible, the lives of the saints, liturgical practices, the economic and political history of the church, the great councils, the writings of theologians, the reflections of reformers, customs, folklore, and local practices.

Of course, the richness of heritage also means clutter. So there must be a way of sorting out the tradition, distinguishing the center from the margins, the dispensable from the unshakeable, the gift from the wrapping. The church community has always accorded the Bible, and within the Bible the New Testament, and within the New Testament the Gospels a special place. Therefore the relating of our personal lives to the tradition often takes the form of a dialogue with scripture. This does not mean we leap over the intervening centuries in the hopes of contacting some pristine Christian experience. It means we appropriate our entire history in terms of how it has embodied the perspectives and values of the charter documents of faith. The contemporary church shuttles back and forth from the records of past living to the problems of present living.

Although the interchange between person and tradition can go on in a one-to-one setting—a person reading the bible alone, a person at prayer, an interpersonal discussion of faith—it is richer and more powerful when done in a group setting. When Christians gather to discern the meaning of their faith—whether accompanied by liturgy or not—the interaction with one another is the experience of church. The outcome of this interactive group process is never predictable. Things happen. Insights occur which would not occur without the dynamics of the group. People gather with the tradition and their own lives; and out of the interaction new possibilities are envisioned which independently could not be seen. When this happens and the awareness of the group is that they are responding to a reality they share but which is greater than they are, they talk about the movement of the Spirit.

Within any group of Christians the actual interaction of personal experience and traditional wisdom is so intricate that it defies thorough analysis. But a broad sketch of the dialogue, a flow chart of mutual influence, is possible. The primary locale where tradition and experience meet is the blood and bones of each person. On the one hand, both genetically and culturally we are walking traditions. Each person is a carrier of inherited convictions and values, not a carbon copy of what went before but a reflection of concerns which have occupied people of the past. On the other hand, we become who we are in our here-and-now interactions with our interpersonal and social environments. Each person is an innovator of insights and attitudes, not a totally new reality but a unique embodiment of the human. Kierkegaard's remark that we understand life backwards but live it forwards and McLuhan's one-liner about driving into the future looking through the rear view mirror capture the interactional flow of tradition and experience in each of us.

Yet within the church community at large, and often within any small group of Christians, there are members who spend the major amount of their time understanding the convictions, feelings, and behaviors of those who preceded us. They tend to stress the continuity between our lives and those of our ancestors. These people are not guardians of the tradition, for that would imply they are defenders of what other people want to plunder. Nor are they the teachers of the tradition, for that would imply other people are there to be taught and not listened to. They are one partner in the dialogue.

Also within the church community at large, and always within small groups of Christians, there are people who spend the majority of their time on the streets and in the neighborhoods, in the city halls and council meetings, in the effort to solve the ongoing problems and celebrate the ongoing hopes. They tend to stress the discontinuity between our lives and those of our ancestors. These people are not in touch with "real life" for that would imply the people of the tradition are in touch with unreal life. These people are not "the pragmatic decision makers" for that would imply the history of previous decisions has nothing to teach us. They are one partner in the dialogue.

In the conversation between experience and tradition two fundamental moves can be readily discerned. First, a concern of contemporary living searches the tradition for perspectives and values which resonate with it. People are never neutral. They consult the tradition out of selective interests. Initially these interests act as filters, allowing in whatever is recognized as a friendly contribution and blocking what appears to be either irrelevant or threatening. A contemporary interest in ecstatic experiences picks up the Christian themes of God's good creation, the resurrection of Jesus, the sending of the Spirit, and the "speaking in tongues" of the early church. The ongoing problems of liturgical renewal look to the history of cultic worship, the importance of meal in the ministry of Jesus, and the sacramental emphasis of the early church. The awareness of social, economic, and political injustice sensitizes us to the Exodus story of liberation, the political bite of Jesus' message, and the ideological mechanisms of all our doctrines and theologies. In the first moment we prosecute the tradition to see if it has anything to say to our concerns.

The second move is that the tradition talks back. For the most part it says, "Yes, but . . . ." The tradition affirms the insights and values that are genuinely Christian but contextualizes them with other insights and values. The tradition offers direct critique when it spots a conviction (we have no reason to hope) or a value (hoarding the goods of the earth) which is directly contrary to the Christian vision. But its more creative mode of challenge is to critique by expansion. It widens the scope of the concern and so makes possible a new approach to it. To the affirmation of ecstatic experiences which have the backing of creation, resurrection, and spirit is added the consideration of fall, crucifixion, and sin. Yes, liturgy is central to the Christian way of life but what was it again that the prophets said about cult? Yes, we must be actively engaged in the political, social, and economic spheres but this involvement stems from belief in God; and this belief means we enter the struggle in a specific way. In the dialogue between experience and tradition experience selects, tradition responds, and the conversation begins to move.

The tradition is an enriching partner in the dialogue. From its purview, the affirmation of the second chapter that our relationship to the transcendent Mystery is gracious, is a bare bones remark. It is the impoverished type of analysis people engage in who do not know they have a past. There have been many revelation-faith experiences and many faith formulations. The tradition has crystallized many of these formulations and has made them a part of our ongoing heritage. Through the symbol of creation we learn that our relationship to Mystery is one of dependency yet partnership. Through the symbol of fall we understand our relationship to Mystery as deeply flawed. Through the symbol of judgment we understand the relationship in terms of its critique of our lack of response. Through the symbols of heaven, hell and kingdom we envision the final future of this relationship. In the matter of our relationship to God the tradition takes our single syllables and turns them into paragraphs.

The very fact we are engaged in dialogue betrays a prejudice in favor of the tradition. We are wagering that the faith formulations of the past can have revelatory power in the present. Although the formulations arose out of specific historical events and are freighted with the language and thought categories of a previous age, they point to an everlasting relationship, our relationship to the ultimate meaning of the Mystery we dwell within. The hope is that they can function, in the language of John Macquarrie, as repetitive revelation.[4] They are the expressions of the revelation-faith experiences of those who came before us. The question is whether they can communicate that experience in such a way that it becomes ours. In this way the formulation has repetitive power. It can evoke the experience that gave it birth. When a traditional faith formulation is able to do this, it is functioning symbolically. We are moving through the faith formulation into our relationship to God and appropriating that relationship in terms of the feelings and perceptions the formulation embodies. If the tradition is able to do this, it is alive. Its formulations are more than accounts of dead people's experiences. They become one of the ways the living touch and interpret the reality that sustains them.

The result of the dialogue between contemporary experience and inherited formulations is the creation of meaning. What comes about is a Christian perspective, a way of inhabiting the present that is faithful to both the Christian vision and the exigencies of the situation. It must be kept in mind that the meaning which emerges is a human construction. It is formulated by people and shot through with both their folly and their greatness. Although its ambition is to express and communicate the movement of God in human life, it can never have pretensions to absolute divine approbation. The sanctioning of our humanly constructed meanings by subtly suggesting they are God's and not ours is a total misreading of the processes of revelation and faith. We are people about the business of discerning the gifts and demands of our relationship to God. It is one of the tasks creatures engage in to pass the time; and so no matter how confident we are about our conclusions, we must heed the oldest of religious warnings. These people call things divine that are merely human.

When Christians gather to remember and hope, they fundamentally engage in a storytelling process. The stories of individual participants, the stories abroad in the culture and the sacred stories of the tradition are interwoven in original and provocative ways. But this ecclesial process is much more than mere story sharing. The stories are part of a total conversational reality. The discussion "hops" from acknowledgements of God to master images that guide our lives to insights which are central to our thinking to values which we prize or abhor to implications which seem appropriate and strategies which appear possible. But the linguistic form which launches the conversation, continues to move it in new directions, and keeps it tied to the concrete world of resistance and possibility is story.

Story is central to group dynamics for two very unspectacular reasons. First, stories are interesting. Alfred North Whitehead once remarked: "In the real world, it is more important that a proposition be interesting than that it be true. The importance of truth is, that it adds to interest."[5] When a story is at full potential, both teller and hearer are engrossed.

The teller is so involved that he or she is merging with the tale. Gertrude Stein has shrewdly observed:

> Everybody's life is full of stories: . . . What is interesting is the way everyone tells their stories. If you listen, really listen, you will hear people repeating themselves. You will hear their pleading nature or their attacking nature or their asserting nature.[6]

Hearers also move from observers to participants. They are suddenly within the story. Amos Wilder thinks this was a dominant characteristic of the stories of Jesus.

> The hearer not only learns about that reality, he participates in it. He is invaded by it. Here lies the power and fatefulness of art. Jesus' speech had the character not of instruction and ideas but of compelling imagination, of spell, of mythical shock and transformation.[7]

Of course, not all storytelling matches the impact of Jesus' stories. But, in general, story is the most interesting and compelling of language forms.

Secondly, stories are accessible. Many people feel out of their depth with heavy conceptual language or abstract psychological discussions. But all people tell stories and listen to them. To ask what someone's values are is often to be greeted by silence; but to ask them to tell of a time when they felt "on the line" is to reach the question of values through the world of story. The mystery of story is that everyone is one and everyone has some; and in a conducive setting everyone wants to tell them.

There are deeper reasons for the prominent role

of story. Stephen Crites argues that all experience is inescapably temporal.[8] Each moment is a "tensed unity" of past, present and future. Therefore, the linguistic form most appropriate to this basic given of human existence is narrative. In fact, in order for life to be creatively negotiated, a person must live out of a narrative infrastructure. Even philosophers, like Sartre, who proclaim a meaningless existence where each moment is alien to every other, are secretly supported by a narrative pattern which enables them to courageously accept that existence.[9] Narrative is an inherent quality of experience and so a primal form of human discourse. Therefore, if theistic faith is to be rooted in experience, it seems it will have a preference for expressing itself in story.

Besides this basic anthropological consideration, storytelling has a specific religious dimension. Sam Keen has remarked that "telling stories is functionally equivalent to belief in God."[10] The very act of storytelling is an implicit affirmation of ultimate meaning. Storytelling raises us out of the randomness of the moment and inserts us into a larger framework. It points to what is holy and sacred which is now defined as "that irreducible principle, power or presence which is the source and guarantor of unity, dignity, meaning, value and wholeness."[11] Charles Winquest philosophically elaborates this insight by contrasting the act and content of storytelling. "What is absent in many modern stories is a *content* of positive affirmation. What is present even in relating a story of nothingness is a positive *act* of affirmation. . . . The escape from meaninglessness is achievable through the transcendence of act over content."[12] True existential atheism is not telling a godless story but having no story to tell.

Also the fact that the sacred writings of Christianity are so heavily story-laden points to the central role of story in religious self-understanding. Whether the traditional stories are historical or fictional is an important consideration but not an all determining one. Both historical accounts (David and Bathsheba) and fictional accounts (the creation of the world) have the intention of truth. They are stories meant to disclose aspects of our relationship to God and through that relationship our commitments to each other. The stories of scripture were remembered and today remain memorable because they are similar enough to our own lives for us to see ourselves, yet different enough from our lives for us to see new possibilities. They tell us what we want to know and more. They come close to home and yet are an invitation to journey. Robert McAfee Brown has said: "A story . . . must reach me on some level to which I can respond, but it must also 'stretch' me, pull me beyond where I am now."[13] The traditional stories, both historical and fictional, reflect concerns and conflicts present in our lives and suggest ways of dealing with them.

Christians are gathered around the table with the book, the bread, and the wine. Their conversation is a rich mixture of contemporary experience and traditional wisdom, with stories a continual and controlling factor. The exact flow of the discussion cannot be captured but, as in chapter one with the process of revelation and faith, some of the logical elements can be pointed at and commented on. These elements are placed in developmental sequence. One leads to two, two suggests three, etc. The value in this is to see a coherent whole, and at least one way the pieces might fit. But in the actual give and take of conversation this sequence is never followed. Anyone who has been involved in Christian reflection groups knows that even when general guidelines are agreed upon, the conversation, like Topsy, just grows.

(1) People relate stories of coming to faith. These are tales in which the initiative of God is stressed. (2) Within these stories the reality of God is acknowledged and God language enters into the conversation. (3) A felt-perception of how the reality of God relates to us is expressed and conveyed in images. (4) The images generate further stories which explore the relationship. (5) These stories yield insights and values. (6) The insights and values have implications. They push toward strategy and action. (7) The faith-motivated behavior yields another set of stories, the stories of enacted faith. Within each element of this basic storytelling process which creates the event of church experience and tradition are simultaneously at work.

Seven Elements

(1) *Stories of coming to faith.* These stories relate either initial experiences of God or times of renewed contact that were especially powerful. Especially powerful contact with God produces a radical shift in our thinking, feeling, and acting. In these stories

the initiative of God plays a dominant role. The stories entail what happened to people more than what people made happen. Often the stories arise from ecstatic experiences like the Sunday vision of Annie Dillard or depth experiences where we definitely feel we are addressed from beyond. The usual pattern of the telling of these stories is, "One day I . . ." and "Since then I . . ." The stories in William James' *Varieties of Religious Experience* fit into this category.

Biographies and autobiographies are filled with these stories. An honored example is that of Francis of Assisi. As he passed by the church of St. Domiono, he felt compelled to go inside. An image of the crucified Christ spoke to him, "Francis, go repair my house, the which, as thous seest, is falling into decay." From that day on Francis began to work untiringly for the reform of the church. Experiences which fund the religious personality give rise to stories of coming to faith. There is also the hint that when these stories are retold, the inexhaustible power of the experience returns.

When the emphasis is on renewed contact with God rather than a first meeting, the person will often connect their experience with a story from the tradition. A friend of mine says the story of Jesus walking on the water has immense significance for her. It is fascinating to hear her retell the story and to retrieve the circumstances under which the story began to become important. Nobody tells an inherited story the same way. They add or subtract, emphasize and de-emphasize to bring out the particular meaning that is significant for them. When my friend retells the story of Jesus walking on the water, the elements of Matthew's story are present; but they are put in a particular context, shaded in a particular way so that Jesus' walking on the water is in some way her own. Also when she tells about the events that were going on in her life when the Jesus of the unruly waves became prominent, the story obviously becomes a tale of the touch of God. Stories of coming to faith relate times when we have been shaken, caressed, or called by God.

(2) *A central moment in all stories of coming to faith is the acknowledgment of God and the consequent ongoing use of God language.* The stories contain the recognition that life is lived in relationship to a transcendent Mystery and that this relationship is of surpassing importance. The recognition and significance of this relationship is conveyed by the word "God."

God language is indispensable for any Christian conversation about life. When it is missing both the personal and transcendent dimensions of the Mystery are often neglected. Substituted language for the brief, blunt impact of "God" is, in the last analysis, too bland. We have been using the parallel "the graciousness of immanent-transcendent Mystery." This is not meant as a replacement for the word "God." It is rather an attempt to disclose the experiential base of God language and so re-habilitate the word. But the more telling obser-vation is not whether God language is used or not, but what is the context of its use. What is the fun-damental imagination of the people with the word

God in their mouths. In general, a supernaturalistic and sacramental imagination can be contrasted.

In the supernaturalistic imagination "God" is a flat, descriptive word. It points to a Supreme Being. We have a relationship with this Supreme Being, and we can understand this relationship through the use of analogy. As we have relationships with other people, so we have a relationship with God. In our relationships with one another our love is mixed with jealousy, our justice is mixed with ignorance, our hope is mixed with desperation. But in our relationship with God we expand what is positive and negate what is negative. So God's relationship to us is all loving, all just and all hopeful. "God loves me" is similar to "Joan loves me," without all the imperfections Joan and I bring to the relationship.

This way of imagining Divine reality and of using God language has some severe limitations. The first difficulty, as every child knows, is that God does not have a body. Yet, he is addressed as if he were another being. Therefore, he must be an invisible Supreme Being. With this initial imaginative structure, faith tends to become believing in someone we do not see. Prayer becomes speaking to the Invisible One. But once again, since the Invisible One has no larynx, no voice speaks back. Prayer, then, is beset by the fear it may be a monologue. In the British movie *The Ruling Class*, Peter O'Toole played a madman who thought he was God. When asked why he thought this, he reasoned, "I must be because I find when I pray, I'm talking to myself." The fact that divine reality is invisible is, in itself, no barrier to communication. However, when the supernaturalistic imagination pictures the invisible God as something like H. G. Wells' invisible man, only bigger, the problems of the silence of God begin.

Secondly, this imagination leads to a literalistic expectation of divine activity. If God is all good and all powerful, he/she will certainly intervene to bring about goodness; for if I were all good and all powerful, I would certainly intervene to bring about goodness. We look to God to act as we do, as one agent in the world. This not only undermines divine transcendence, for God is the source and destiny of all activity and not one more instance of it, but it also generates pseudo problems. When we do not see God acting in this way, we proclaim the death of the divine. We say we have lost faith. But what has really happened is that a too literalistic imagination has stimulated an expectation which is a fantasy. The real tragedy is not that God does not intervene, but that we overlook the God who cannot intervene because he is already there.

Thirdly, the Invisible One, who could intervene but does not, naturally tends to be the "man upstairs." God is basically missing and all energies must be spent on the times and places he mysteriously makes contact with us. Contact with the absent God usually occurs through messengers. In the Christian tradition he sent angels, prophets, and in the fullness of time his Son, Jesus Christ. We believe on the word of these messengers. Their testimony becomes our faith. We have not personally touched this God but others have, and they have told us about him. The tendency in this imagination is to focus on the special times and places as the only sources of revelation.

The Event of the Church and the Stories of Faith

Since we do not experience this God, the best we can do is to guard and pass on what the special people have said.

This is a broad brush caricature of the supernaturalistic mode of talking about God. On the level of thought we can check the misleading tendencies of this imagination. We can stress the limits of analogy with personal relationships, combining the way of affirmation and the way of negation in talking about God. We can develop theories of primary and secondary causality to deal with divine activity. We can complement special revelation with an understanding of the universal pressence of God and the continuing sacramental experience of the special revelatory events. But imagination is an orientation toward reality more fundamental than thinking. It has tendencies which pull us in a certain direction; and although the mind may pinpoint the problems and try to solve them, it cannot change the direction. In another image, if the imagination has a gaping hole, thinking will not patch it for long. In a final image, imagination is the room and thinking is the furniture. We may move the furniture from corner to corner to get new and fascinating looks. But sometimes what is needed is a larger room.

In the sacramental imagination "God" is most properly used in the vocative. God is a word people call out when they come into contact with the Greater Than They Are. William Luijpen gives some examples of this use of God language.

> A child is born and the religious man exclaims, "God!" In health or illness the religious man shouts, "God!" He is

dying and his lips whisper, "God!" When he is reduced to slavery in Egypt, rises against his oppressors, overcomes the terrible risk of his revolt against his masters, a religious man exclaims, "God!" The religious man calls, shouts, whispers the name "God!" He prays, he sings, he shouts for joy and lament, he sorrows and curses.[14]

In the movie *Close Encounters of the Third Kind* a magnificent space ship suddenly appears over the top of the mountain. The technicians, who have gathered on the mountain, look up and are stunned. "Oh God, Oh God," they mutter in amazement. Obviously, the spaceship is not God. But in and through their reaction to the spaceship they acknowledge a greater Mystery within which they live but which is much more than they are. The story is told of a twenty-two-year-old girl, blind from birth, who had an eye transplant. When the bandages were removed, she opened her eyes. "The more she now directed her gaze upon everything about her, the more it could be seen how an expression of gratification and astonishment overspread her features. She repeatedly exclaimed, 'Oh God, how beautiful.' "[15] The girl does not see God. She sees color, but in the interaction between herself and the colorful objects of the room she is triggered into an awareness of the greater Mystery she lives within. She signals that awareness by calling, "God."

But the word God is not left as an exclamation. We move it from the vocative to the nominative case. "God" becomes the subject of a sentence. The reason for this is that the felt perception of our relationship to Mystery is that it initiates the relationship. In order to communicate this felt perception, we make God the subject of the sentence. The subject of a sentence is an agent, the one who is acting. To start a sentence with "God" is simply to state the fundamental dynamic of the relationship. The referent in experience for "God" as subject is completely different than the referent in experience for "Joan" as subject. At this moment we are not engaged in analogy but in linguistically expressing the felt perception that the Mystery instigates all interaction.

With God as the subject of a sentence, verbs and objects quickly follow. In the sacramental imagination when we say "God is love," we do not mean, in the first instance, that love is an inherent quality of God. We mean our *relationship* to God is loving. God language is always self-involving. We cannot talk about the Mystery independent of our relationship to it. At this moment we are involved in a form of analogy but not in a transfer of qualities from one relationship to another. We do not "hop" from a relationship to others and back again. We know divine love through the experience of human love, but we are not setting up the equation: as in my relationship with others I have experienced love so in my relationship with God I experience a love somewhat the same and somewhat different.

The sacramental imagination always keeps the reality and presence of God joined to the reality and presence of the finite world. In and through our love for one another we become aware of a greater Love which supports and encourages us. In the sacramental imagination, God, self, and others are permanently bound together. We cannot talk about our relationship with God without talking about our finite relationships; and we cannot talk about our finite relationships at any depth without talking about our relationship to God. In other words, the experience behind the phrase "God is Love" is a human relationship which is so loving that it touches upon a source of love that so inexhaustibly funds it that the people involved call out, "God is love!"

The sacramental imagination begins with the bias of a universal divine presence. The question is not how to make the missing God present but how does the ubiquitous God enter into mind and heart? Faith is not believing in what cannot be seen but responding in mind, heart and action to what cannot be escaped. The sacramental imagination makes God language a unique mode of expression. Although it uses ordinary words, it does not function like everyday langauge. Within the sacramental imagination God language avoids some of the alienating qualities it displays within the supernaturalistic imagination. But whatever imagination is at work, difficulties arise. The question is: which imagination initially provides a more powerful approach to ultimate reality?

A favorite story about the contrast between the supernaturalistic and sacramental imagination is the tale of the old man and the young priest. It is the late fifties and the Russians have put a man in space. On his return the cosmonaut informs the world that he has been to the house of God and no one was home. He has been to the far reaches of space and no God greeted him. The old man on Chicago's West side is perturbed about this and consults the newly ordained parish priest. "What about what this Commie said?" The priest, fresh from a reading of Paul Tillich, explains that heaven is really a symbol for the transcendence of God. God does not literally live in the sky. God is present everywhere, and we use the symbol of the sky to talk about the transcendent Mystery of God. "Ha!" said the old man with a disgusted look on his face, "The son of a bitch didn't fly high enough."

(3) *Images.* When God language enters the conversation, images are not far behind. Since the reality of God has an impact on the total person, the language that emerges from that experience is as holistic as possible. Images have both cognitive and affective power. Through the image we *know* something about the relationship to God, but we also have *"some feel"* for what it is like to live in that relationship. This rounded ability make images an appropriate first form to convey the experience of God.

In the Christian tradition God has many images. Divine reality is a person, a father, mother, husband, lover, friend, shepherd, farmer, dairymaid, laundress, builder, potter, fisherman, tradesman, physician, teacher, scribe, nurse, metalworker, king, warrior, judge, rock, fortress, mighty river, fire, and whirlwind.[16] The multiplicity of images suggests the basic structure of the relationship. We are in relationship to a transcendent reality. This reality cannot be captured in one image or in all the images clustered together. The veto on images in the Old Testament is a reminder that the full reality of God is always beyond our reach. Yet this reality which our images cannot exhaust is able to be contacted through them. This paradox, an imageless God available through images, is at the heart of the sacramental imagination.

Images of God are often taken from the very medium of disclosure. For example, a person gazes at the sky and has a disclosure experience, a moment when he becomes aware of the transcendent Mystery. He instinctively says, "Heavenly God." The disclosure came through his interaction with the sky and he uses the sky to convey the meaning of transcendence. Another example would be interpersonal love. In the experience of loving someone a person becomes aware of a transpersonal source, a true Otherness which legitimates and encourages her feelings and behaviors. Therefore, to focus this illusive presence she linguistically "separates it out" and names it with the feelings, attitudes and values through which it entered her awareness. God is a lover. This process of the sacramental imagination seems particularly suited to parent imagery. It is in and through the experiences of fatherhood and motherhood that the Mystery of divine reality as generating love enters human awareness. Therefore, it is only natural that mother and father become the main images of God.

Although images are often taken from the medium through which the Mystery was encountered, more often they are chosen because they accurately convey the felt perception of the relationship. The experience of the relationship is logically prior to the images. So various images can be tried out to see if they capture the nuances of the relationship. In the Book of Kings, Elijah is ordered outside his cave to watch the Lord pass by. The writer then uses the images of a mighty wind, an earthquake, and a fire; but God is in none of these images. Finally, a small, whispering sound carries the presence of God. Through the imagery the writer is discounting some felt perceptions about the relationship to God and focusing on the one that is true for him in that situation. The use of imagery is dictated by what is happening in the relationship to God.

Also, diverse images can be used to convey the same meaning. The psalmist calls God a "rock" and Father Mapple, in Melville's *Moby Dick*, calls God the "sure Keel of the Ages." Both the psalmist and the preacher are communicating the same felt perception. To live in this relationship is to find a security beyond what the finite world can offer. But they are using different metaphors derived from different environments to convey this felt perception.

When Christians gather, images drawn from the inherited writings merge with images of contemporary experience. The result is a baffling originality. On one hand, it is the personal appropriation of the traditional faith; and on the other, it is the enlivening of the traditional faith by personal experience. In the quotation which opens this chapter, Edith Sitwell's old people combine the broken window of a slum with the burning bush and the crumb for a starving bird with the broken Body of Christ. In the following paragraph from Annie

Dillard, the traditional images of cross and crib are merged with the image of diver to talk about the reality of God's presence to human life.

> Faith would be that God is self-limited utterly by his creation—a contraction of the scope of his will; that he bound himself to time and its hazards and hopes as a man would lash himself to a tree for love. That God's works are as good as we make them. That God is helpless, our baby to bear, self-abandoned on the doorstep of time, wondered at by cattle and oxen. Faith would be that God moved and moves once for all and 'down,' so to speak, like a diver, like a man who eternally gathers himself for a dive and eternally is diving, and eternally splitting the spread of the water, and eternally drowned.[17]

In the poetry of Brother Antoninius God images are also both traditional and personal. At one moment God is imaged as "the great eye," "a dog," and "a slave." At the next he is the loving father, the phoenix, Christ eternal, the lover. And in this contemporary prayer the blending of scriptural images and images drawn from contemporary life display how the experience of God is talked about.

> Lord God,
> the never knifed bleed words
> and come to you
> out of the rush hour traffic
> with bumper-to-bumper syllables,
> chatting about how their day went,
> standing you in the kitchen with a drink
> while they putter with supper.
>
> But the ones who fear
> holy ground burns shoes

lurk in the shadows of thurible smoke
with some tongueless pain or love.
as silent as Zachary
before the birth of John,
each day rephrasing what they will say
and each night knowing it can only be,
"Blessed be God."

And then there are nomad hearts
camping and decamping in desert storms.
the hope of a milk and honey home
long abandoned.
The cool water of your words,
Lord God,
has turned to the sand of search.
the high romance of pilgrimage
now only the fierce determination
to go on.[18]

Traditional and contemporary images stand side by side not only in written material but also in conversation. In workshops on the experience of God the participants are asked to retrieve a time when they were acutely aware that they were related to something greater than themselves. The retrieval focuses on the concrete circumstances and the feelings of the experience. Once these feelings are fairly well articulated the leader asks what it felt "like." The following is a verbatim from one participant:

As I said, it was scary yet OK. Like I was on a rotor, those things at amusement parks that go around at top speed, and then the bottom falls out. You are pinned to the side and everyone is screaming from fright, but nobody is really frightened. It was like that. The bottom was out but

I knew I wouldn't fall. I was held, you know, safe in the arms of God, like when the father embraced the prodigal son.

Another example reveals the same dynamic:

I felt peace like I was a study overflowing with papers, not neat but loving. Nothing was quite in place yet nothing was lost. I've felt like that before, after my second baby. Like Mary I treasured things in my heart.

One value of the tradition is that it gives us a language for the depth of our present experiences. One value of our present experiences is it revitalizes the language of our tradition.

Although there seem to be no rules for how personal and traditional images should interact, a general assessment is possible in terms of the tasks of God language. The theorists of religion assign at least three functions to God talk. God talk names the intention of the Mystery toward all that dwell within it. But, as we have emphasized, it is people who speak of God so there is always a self-involving aspect. God talk is performative. It expresses the commitment of the speaker to the values contained in the language. But beyond the naming and commitment functions, God language is supposed to be evocative. Since it was born in a disclosure experience and its personal meaning depends on an awareness of the relationship revealed in that experience, its use should bring Mystery to mind and heart. In other words, it should not only talk about our relationship to Mystery; it should evoke the presence of Mystery. For some thinkers adjectives such as all-loving, or everlasting, or immutable are attempts, through radical qualifiers, to encourage this awareness. When God talk is at its best, it is naming the Mystery, expressing our commitment to it and evoking its presence.

In general, the inherited images function to name the Mystery and express our commitment to it but are unable to evoke its presence. The simple fact that the images have been around so long and have become so much a part of ordinary parlance means they cannot shock us out of our everyday perceptions. They are not innovative enough. They are permanent metaphors for our convictions and values but not live metaphors for our experience. They stabilize our thinking and feeling but seldom excite us. They function as the rudder, not the sail.

When contemporary Christians say "Our Father who art in heaven," they name the heart of the Mystery as loving and commit themselves to it. But the felt relationship to Mystery seldom enters mind and heart in the speaking of the words. At the time of Jesus there are indications that it might have been different. The dominant consciousness of the time was that God was utterly transcendent. Yet the image of Abba (Father) connotes intimacy and closeness. This reverses the initial expectation of reverence and distance; then quickly re-affirms it with, "who art in heaven." This juxtaposition of near yet far, intimate yet majestic, loving yet awesome is the type of poetic contrast that does more than name and express; it invokes the natural presence of the Mystery for those who hear the words and for those who speak them. But the original situation of Jesus and his friends is not ours. The potential of certain God images at that time is not the potential they have today. When an image becomes firmly established in the tradition, it often loses its evocative impact at the same time that its expressive and naming functions are heightened.

This general guideline—that inherited images name our relationship to Mystery and express our commitment to it while personal images evoke the presence of Mystery—can be seen by contrasting Psalm 148 with a poem by Anne Sexton.

> Praise the Lord from the heavens,
>   praise him in the heights;
> Praise him, all you his angels,
>   praise him, all you his hosts.
> Praise him, sun and moon;
>   praise him, all you shining stars.
> Praise him, you highest heavens,
>   and you waters above the heavens
> Let them praise the name of the LORD,
>   for he commanded and they were
>   created;
> He established them forever and ever;
>   he gave them a duty which shall not
>   pass away.
>
> Praise the LORD from the earth,
>   you sea monsters and all depths;
> Fire and hail, snow and mist,
>   storm winds that fulfill his word;
> You mountains and all you hills,
>   you fruit trees and all you cedars;
> You wild beasts and all tame animals,
>   you creeping things and you winged
>   fowl.

The Event of the Church and the Stories of Faith

Let the kings of the earth and
    peoples,
    the princes and all the judges of
    earth,
Young men too, and maidens,
    old men and boys,
Praise the name of the LORD,
    for his name alone is exalted;
His majesty is above earth and heaven
    and he has lifted up the horn of
    people.
Be this his praise from all his faithful ones,
    from the children of Israel,
        people close to him.

And now "Welcome Morning" by Anne Sexton.

There is joy
in all:
in the hair I brush each morning,
in the Cannon towel, newly washed,
that I rub my body with each morning,
in the chapel of eggs I cook
each morning,
in the outcry from the kettle
that heats my coffee
each morning,
in the spoon and the chair
that cry "hello there, Anne"
each morning,
in the godhead of the table
that I set my silver, plate, cup upon
each morning.

All this is God,
right here in my pea-green house
each morning
and I mean,

107

though often forget,
to give thanks,
to faint down by the kitchen table
in a prayer of rejoicing
as the holy birds at the kitchen window
peck into their marriage of seeds.

So while I think of it,
let me paint a thank-you on my palm
for this God, this laughter of the morning,
lest it go unspoken.

The Joy that isn't shared, I've heard,
dies young.[19]

Psalm 148 carries the convictions and values of
praise, but it is doubtful if it has the power to bring
the reader, listener or speaker to the experience of
praise. Sexton's poem has a better chance. By themselves the traditional images are prone to convictions without inspiration; by themselves contemporary images are prone to enthusiasm without direction.

Images are a very explosive linguistic form. When
they are introduced into conversation, the pace of
the discussion is instantly quickened. Images play
upon the experiences of the people and call forth
many responses. A recent workshop on ministry and
spirituality was going its usual, somewhat bland
route when one of the ministers said that he looked
at what he did as a cross between a shotgun and a
shepherd's staff. Another chimed in that he thought
his ministry was more like a baton. A third said he
liked to think of his church as a round table. Once
these images were introduced into the discussion, it

galvanized the participants; and a rich and in-depth analysis of ministry was begun. Images have tremendous power to trigger multiple human responses.

The very richness and power of imagery is also the source of its problems. The image is open-ended and so capable of being developed in many different directions. To call God a father could be taken to mean that ultimate reality is male. Therefore, females are second class citizens in relationship to the Mystery of human life. Or if we are working out of a heavy Freudian mythology, it could be quickly concluded that the father god must be killed in order for the sons to gain prominence. Or if our personal history with our own father was rocky, the image may convey the sense of God's lack of care and concern, that the relationship is indifferent. To call God a king can lead us to think that God rules the world in a sovereign fashion and that we are mere serfs and not partners in the governing. It could give the impression that God lives in the royal city of heaven and only occasionally visits the outlying districts of earth. To call God a creator could lead to the deist idea that he is a clock maker. Having set the world in motion, he now sits back and watches it tick. Also it could be twisted to mean that our actions are insignificant compared to the grandeur of God's creative activity. The evocative power of imagery has little control over what it evokes.

Our tradition calls God a father, a king, and a creator. These images not only communicate, they overcommunicate. They have a tendency to say more than they want to. They carry the felt perception of the relationship but they can also distort the felt perception. Because of this, images are never enough. Stories must be told which initially tighten and direct the image.

(4) *Stories of exploring faith.* In the first moment stories delimit the possibilities of the image. They restrict its open-ended potential and give it a particular direction. Jesus calls God a father and then tells the story of the prodigal father. Among other things the prodigal father is the systematic repudiation of patriarchy. Three times in the story the father goes against the existing customs of patriarchial privilege. He divides his money between his sons; he runs to greet the lost son; and he comes out of his house to urge the older brother to join the party. These three gestures contradict the unwritten laws of patriarchy. No father would give his money away and put himself in a position of possible destitution. Joachim Jeremias says that it is extremely undignified for an aged oriental to run, but run this father does. For the older son not to attend the party is a classic insult; but for the father to come out and try to coax him in is an unprecedented gesture. With the story of the prodigal father as a guide, the image of God as father cannot be used as a buttress for the patriarchial system.

The meaning of the kingship of God is also sharpened by the stories Jesus tells. God cannot be imaged as a sovereign non-involved reality when Jesus' stories of God's kingship talk about human well-being and human transformation. Nor can God as king mean harsh judgment when Jesus tells the story of the king who forgives the servant the great debt. Nor can the kingship of God mean the exclusion of the sinner when Jesus' table fellowship with the outcasts is a sign of the presence of that kingdom. Jesus' parables gradually shape the meaning of the image of king. It seems that Jesus was initially warmly received because he used the popular image of king. But once his stories focused the meaning of God's kingship, he was rejected by the authorities and many of his countrymen. Stories restrict images and begin the movement toward clarity.

The stories in the first two chapters of Genesis direct the image of God as creator. It is difficult to hold that God is a creator who keeps power to himself when the stories talk about his empowering the man and the woman to tend to the garden and care for one another. It is difficult to talk about dependency on God when the story talks about human responsibility.

The story which initially delimits the meaning of the image subsequently expands it. It does this primarily by triggering other stories. The story of the prodigal father evokes other stories of fatherhood, both personal and inherited, which seem to be "of one piece" with it. The stories of transformation and forgiveness which specify the image of king lead to other stories of transformation and forgiveness. The story of a creator who empowers and calls forth naturally elicits tales of empowerment and responsibility. Many of the stories that are called forth by the original story use new imagery. It is not uncommon for the story of the prodigal father to prod someone to tell a story of their mother. The story of the forgiving king easily moves to the story of the forgiving husband. What happens in this process is a gradual unfolding, not only of our relationship to God but also of what people look like when they are participating to a high degree in that relationship. The stories that clarify the open-endedness of the image are themselves open-ended. They simultaneously contract and expand the discussion.

But stories do more than trigger other stories. They also suggest insights and elicit action. All three types of response—story, insight, and action—were present when this rendition of an ancient Hassidic tale was told.

There was a poor rabbi who lived in the city of Krakow. He lived on the street of the Lost Angel, in the last hovel on that street, with his wife and his four children. Since he was extremely poor, he dreamed every night of riches. But one night the dream was exceptionally vivid. He dreamt that underneath a bridge in the city of Warsaw there was a treasure. When he awoke in the morning, he excitedly told his wife and his children about his dream. He then packed food and clothes, and set off for the long journey to find that bridge, unearth that treasure, and be rich. He traveled many long days and long nights and finally arrived at Warsaw. It was just as the dream had pictured it, except for one thing. There was a guard on the bridge, a sentinel who paced back and forth. And so the poor rabbi, tired from his journey, fell asleep in the bushes. When he awoke, he rattled the bushes with his arm, and the guard spun on him: "You there, come here!" He was a simple man so he did not run. He sheepishly came forward. The guard said, "What are you doing here?" Being a simple man who would not run, he was also a simple man who would not lie. He said, "I have dreamed that underneath this bridge there is a treasure, and I have traveled many long miles to find that treasure and be rich." The guard said, "That is strange! Just last night I, too, have had a dream. I have dreamt that in the city of Krakow, on the street of the Lost Angel, in the last hovel on that street, where lives a rabbi and his wife and their four children there is buried behind the fireplace a treasure. And I leave tonight to find it and be rich."

The responses to that story were very diverse. One person immediately began to distill a meaning. "It seems we always overlook the things that are close. We are so greedy for what we do not have, we do not appreciate what we have." A second reaction was the Canterbury response—one story calls forth another. A woman said, "That's just like my brother. My brother has recently been divorced and that's what he is like. He had a good wife and a fine home, and he was always out on the road." And she began to tell the story of her brother's divorce and her feelings about that.

There was a man in the group who was very quiet but obviously involved. After about a half-hour of discussion on the story and its meaning, the leader turned to the man and said, "How about yourself? What did you think about the story?" The man stood up, said, "I'm going to go call my brother," and walked out of the room. The ultimate response to story is action.

Stories can be inhabited in many different ways. They can be entered on any level that both they and we agree on. Stories allow a freedom and latitude that straightforward discourse discourages. The man who walked out of the room later told the leader that he and his brother had been "on the outs;" and that he felt now was the time to do something about it. The story was able to move him to reconciliation. Exactly how is anybody's guess. But one thing is certain—a moral exhortation on the need for family unity would not have triggered the same response. The story is able to meet us where we are at without clubbing us into where we should be. Although the story focuses our minds and hearts, it does not close them down, demanding we move in only one direction.

As with image, the power of story is also its problem. Its high "trigger" ability means low control. A favorite anecdote of Flannery O'Connor's was about the student who deduced the moral of *The Scarlet Letter* as: Think twice before committing adultery." Stories are not as wide open as images, but they are prey to reductionistic and misleading distillations of meaning. The story of the prodigal father does move us away from male dominance; but it can lead us to the flippant attitude that we can do whatever we want because God is always waiting with open arms. Jesus' story of all the outcasts at the supper of the great king moves us away from an exclusivistic understanding of God's kingship; but it could also encourage us to think there are no requirements for Kingdom living. The creation stories move us away from a "serf" approach; but they could push us to the other extreme and suggest we are the dominant master of all creation. There is need for a further clarification. This need is spontaneously met as people go beyond story to the insights the story contains and the values it proposes.

(5) *Insights and values.* In *Zorba the Greek* Nikos Kazantzakis has the boss say, "If only I could never open my mouth ... until the abstract idea had reached its highest point—and had become a story!"[20] But the stories we have considered are not concrete illustrations of abstract ideas. They are the rawest expression of the tumult of experience. They do not embody the ideas of the mind, but they give rise to ideas as fire gives rise to smoke. In this way the ideas formulated from the story do not replace it. The story is multi-intentional, capable of many interpretations. When it is read or told in different environments, it generates different understandings. The move to insights and values is necessary if we are to arrive at an action which is in accord with the story, which is an interpretation of the image, which carries the felt perception of the relationship to the God whom we have met. But if the story is abandoned, we also are abandoned to the single insight and value which one time and one place distilled from the story.

The way in which a story generates many meanings can be shown from Luke's account of Jesus' story of the cheating accountant. The basic tale starts with: "A rich man had a manager who was reported to him for dissipating his property;" and ends with, "The owner then gave his devious employee credit for being enterprising!" Two interpretations are quickly tacked on. Luke asks why the servant who tampered with the books was applauded and concludes: "Because the worldly take more initiative than the other-worldly when it comes to dealing with their own kind." Leonardo Boff comments on this:

> It is a distressing discovery: Christians will always be in a disadvantageous position in business matters because they cannot employ the illicit methods used by the children of darkness.[21]

Luke then draws a second moral from the story. "What I say to you is this: Make friends for yourselves through your use of this world's goods, so that when they fail you, a lasting reception will be yours." This world's goods, which will surely pass away, should be used to make friends. In Jesus' mouth the point of the parable was probably completely different: the need to act in a crisis. If judgment is coming (the definitive arrival of the Kingdom) and the time is short, we must quickly respond. Within scripture alone the same story has yielded three interpretations.

The lesson of this text is an important one. Although the story exists as a set form in the Book, the Book is in the hands of the people and the people are in the throes of God. It is not the story which formulates the insights and proposes the values, it is the people who hear and read the story. And since the people change, the story is able to work its way into new minds and new hearts with new results. In Luke's full text we have the insights that the way to respond to a crisis is to exercise ingenuity, that cheating is not a Christian option, that wealth will finally fail us; and we have the corresponding values of action over apathy, honesty over fraud, and friendship over money. If, when Christians gather today, the story is read, it will undoubtedly trigger other meanings. They will not be the exact insights or values of either Jesus or Luke. Of course, they must be in general conformity with the scriptural insights, and this is basically assured by the fact that the same story instigated them. But they will also be different, and this is basically assured by the fact that we are neither first century Jews nor hellenistic Christians. The move to insight and value is 'absolutely necessary but it does not mean the elimination of story.

Some of the insights and values which might be derived from the stories which specify our basic images are:

The story of the prodigal father is a story about the overcoming of the past. The son has ostracized himself from his family (by asking for the money before the father had died he was saying in effect, "Die, old man") and his nation (by herding swine he had placed himself in the category of the permanently damned, a "Jew who had made himself a Gentile"). Hungry amid the squalor of pigs and pagans, he is the son who has become sin. In this irredeemable situation he writes the model of all self-hating scripts. "Father, I have sinned before heaven and thee, do not take me back as a son but as a hired hand." The returning one is willing to settle for the status of hired hand, just to work around the place. But no sooner is the script out of his mouth than the father is calling for the robe, ring, sandals, and food of festivity for his son has returned. The old man knows that if the son returns as a hired hand, his sin will ever remain in his throat. Every day the other hired hands will say, "There's the son who blew it." The story says that the experience of God is the possibility of the return to sonship and daughtership after it has been denied. The past does not have to determine the future. The sins of the fifteen-year-old do not have to haunt the thirty-year-old; and the seventy-year-old does not have to die with the failures of his forties. If the question is how to get a better future after we have betrayed what is best about us, the answer is forgiveness; and the story tells us it is available. As a people who tell this story we value possibility over punishment, reconciliation over revenge, forgiveness over grudge.

All of Jesus' parables fill out the image of God's kingship. But the story of the king who gave the great supper picks up a theme of Jesus' total ministry. Although it is a tale of those who accept and those who reject the offer of a feast, it is also significant that the invitation eventually went out to all. Jesus' stories and his actions are often concerned with pulling in the outcasts. The people who were usually pushed away, Jesus pulled toward himself. Prostitutes, tax collectors, children of the street, the poor, lepers, the blind, the lame, the mute, the deaf were all welcome around his table. God's mercy was approaching for all, so all were bound together by the overwhelming fact of God's all encompassing love. When Christians live out of the stories of the kingdom, we value inclusion over exclusion, unity over division, community over privilege.

The Genesis stories of creation are about the

sanctification of all finite reality, our partnership with God, our need for each other, and our kinship with the earth. Creation is real and good but it is not God. All things were made for the Sabbath which is a day of delight. God shares his creative powers with the man and the woman and gives them responsibility for themselves and the garden. The man and woman were once one so the effort to become one again in sexual union is validated. These stories spark many insights and guide us to values of respect for nature over brute manipulation of it, of joy in being finite over despair about not being infinite, of responsibility for each other over looking out for number one.

(6) *Implications.* Implications cover a lot of territory. In the first moment the insights and values become antennae with which we pick up the depth sounds of life. Living out of the forgiving God we become sensitive to situations of alienation, to the way "sin sticks," to the way we rehearse failure till we feel resignation. Out of the conviction of a universal invitation we notice how quickly we exclude and by excluding how we find a perverse self-worth. We are not like *them*. The insights and values of the creation stories direct us to ecological and sexual questions. The insights and values—derived from the stories which explored the image which arose from the recognition of the God who entered our lives at one time—makes us attentive to the areas of life which the reality of God attends to. Through the insights and values we perceive the redemptive patterns of human existence.

But the insights and values do more than sensitize us to what we otherwise might not be aware of. They provide stable attitudes towards the fluctuating situations of life. The forgiving God makes us people of hope. The God who invites all makes us a people leary of our ingrained prejudices and ever open to new forms of community. The creating God encourages in us a respect for all and a delight in all. The insights and values suggest attitudes which provide a basic orientation within life.

The insight and values alert us to certain situations and ground us in certain attitudes; but more fundamentally they push toward concrete embodiment. They unravel into strategies. This movement toward action is never a strict deductive process. Rather the insights and values are consulted in the thinking and planning process, and out of the consultation comes an approach to the situation genuinely influenced by those insights and values. Robert Tannehill in *The Sword of His Mouth* gives an example of how the insights and values of a biblical text guide decision-making and action.

> Let us imagine that the administrator of a social agency is informed that one of his most trusted subordinates has been caught in a serious crime. He reacts with anger. His trust has been betrayed, and those who oppose what the agency is attempting to do among the urban poor now have an excuse for cutting back the agency's funds. In this situation he reads Matt 5:39b-42.
>
> Whoever strikes you on the right cheek,
> Turn to him the other also;
> And for him who would sue you and take your tunic,

Leave for him your cloak as well;
And whoever will force you to walk for one mile,
Go with him two miles.
To him who asks you, give,
And to him who would borrow from you, do not refuse.

Assuming that he takes what he reads seriously, his reactions might pass through the following stages: He may see immediately that these commands are meddling in his business. In terms of vs. 39b, he has been slapped on the cheek. His first reaction to the command may be a deeper anger. This will be accompanied by the feeling that the command is impractical. The one who betrayed him simply cannot be continued in his position and allowed to do the same thing again. After all, an administrator cannot think of one man only; he must think of the many people to whom he is responsible, those above him who dispense funds and the poor whom he is trying to help. However, these strange commands cannot be forgotten. They work at the back of his mind, and as they do, he realizes that at first he had been primarily concerned with himself. He had been angry at this betrayal of his trust and this threat to his treasured program. As he recognizes this, he begins to consider other possible responses: 'Even if I do have to suspend him from his position, there are some other things which can be done. Perhaps my testimony at the trial will help him to receive a suspended sentence. If so, I might be able to help him get a job somewhere.... There is the problem of replacing him, too. Should I look for a safe middle-class fellow or for another "high risk" type? Maybe it is worth running the risk....[22]

Of course, the "turning the other cheek" text is difficult because it so brutally cuts across our natural instincts. But how the administrator worries the text into his decision is the halting way the

Christian vision moves toward action. It is through a process as painful and piecemeal as this that we allow the Christian insights and values to take hold.

David Tracy has outlined more precisely the steps involved in moving from values to action. His specific concern is social ethics but the distinctions apply to any area of human activity.

> There is a well-recognized set of distinctions in contemporary Christian social ethics which bears recalling here: the distinction between general (and usually fairly abstract) ethical principles (love thy neighbor); middle axioms, or ethical dictates which are still relatively general but more concrete (racism is in all circumstances wrong); and finally concrete social ethical policies (the debate on busing as a specific policy to fight against racism).[23]

People of religious faith move from their proximate environments to ultimate reality. But once they have formulated the meaning of their ultimate situation, they move back "down" (so to speak) through all their environments, asking how their ultimate identity and destiny influences all they come in contact with. Each step "out of" God and "into" the world demands more human initiative and more complex ingenuity. The last step is strategy. What will the people of this God do?

On this last level of strategy there are three perennial temptations. The first is not to have strategies. Our minds are convinced God is love and our hearts trust ultimate reality; but we do not struggle with the implications of our convictions and feelings for interpersonal and social living. God is basically an inner experience with very little outer ramifications.

The second temptation is to equate the experience of God with one strategy. To continue Tracy's example, to be against busing is not to believe in a God of love. This is a confusion which often plagues Christian conversations. People may hold the same convictions and values but disagree on how to embody them. But in the heat of the discussion this distinction is often blurred and the accusation is heard: "If you are not for this form of action, you disvalue love and are not Christian." The experience of God and the corresponding values, precisely because they are transcendent, permit multiple strategies.

The third temptation is to engage in strategies that are inappropriate. These actions do not embody the values or only do so to a minimal degree. It is true that every strategy to some extent will be inappropriate. Christian values have an eschatological orientation; so every situation short of the final Kingdom will be incomplete. But the temptation is to settle for an appropriate strategy, not to continue to rethink and redo in the light of our values and the possibilities that come about. But no matter what strategies are adopted, the resistances we meet and the new situations which are created will give rise to stories, stories of enacted faith.

(7) *Stories of enacted faith.* Stories of enacted faith are always life histories.[24] They recount what happens to people when they struggle with God, themselves, and the world. It was these types of

stories that the last part of chapter two was concerned with. Stories of enacted faith always display
the dynamic that John attributes to Jesus.

> Jesus—fully aware that he had come from God and was
> going to God, the father who handed everything over to
> him—rose from the meal, took off his cloak, he picked up a
> towel, tied it around himself. Then he poured water into a
> basin and began to wash his disciples' feet and dry them
> with the towel he had around him.

Moving out of an understanding that the coming and
going of his life was God, Jesus does "the thing" of
God. The structure of the stories of enacted faith is:
"With these convictions and values this is what I did;
this is what happened; this is how I responded."

With these stories we have come full circle. The
God we met in our stories of coming to faith and
investigated in our stories of exploring faith is now
embodied in the stories of enacted faith. But this
does not end the storytelling process. Rather it is the
assurance that more stories are in the offing. For
contact with the God who takes the initiative in our
stories of coming to faith is only maintained when we
take the initiative in our stories of enacted faith. The
way to insure we will meet God again is to act out of
the God we have already met. As Jesus suggests in
the Our Father, the way to continue to experience
the forgiveness of God is to forgive each other. The
stories of enacted faith provide the possibility of a
new meeting with the familiar yet ever strange God.
Out of this new meeting comes a different acknowledgement, a different image, different stories of ex-

ploration, different insights and values, different implications, and different struggles which give rise to new stories of enacted faith. And the journey of faith goes on.

As a Christian people we come to be in the interaction between our personal experience and the traditional wisdom. This exchange is a complex blend of affirmation and challenge; and when we are engaged in it, we are experiencing what it means to be a church. Although acknowledgements, images, insights, values, and implications are essential to this discussion, it is fundamentally a storytelling process. If we forget this, we quickly fly into abstractions or wallow in moralisms. The center of our tradition is appropriately a man of a thousand stories. The story of Jesus' coming to faith is encapsulated in his special word, "Abba." The stories that explore his faith are the unforgetable parables. The story that enacts his faith is his actual life. We must now approach him more directly. For the simple but overwhelming remark of the Epistle to the Hebrews (6:20) cannot be neglected. He is our forerunner.

Chapter Four

The Forerunner of Faith

I never followed Christ's bloody journey to Golgotha with such terror, I never relived his Life and Passion with such intensity, such understanding and love, as during the days and nights when I wrote *The Last Temptation of Christ*. . . . In order to mount to the Cross, the summit of sacrifice, and to God, the summit of immateriality, Christ passed through all the stages which the man who struggles passes through. That is why his suffering is so familiar to us; that is why we share it, and why his final victory seems to us so much our own future victory.[1]

Nikos Kazantzakis

In each individual the spirt has become flesh, in each man the creation suffers, within each one a redeemer is nailed to the cross.[2]

Hermann Hesse

KAZANTZAKIS and Hesse are not alone. The story of Jesus carries the struggles and hopes of all our stories. Jesus was a person of a definite time and place, immersed in history and bounded by the traditions of his people. Yet this radical particularity is not an obstacle to meeting him. In fact, it is the indispensable prerequisite. There is a temptation to think: the more universal, the more accessible. A psychological treatment of family life will be more acceptable than the story of the Prodigal Son. We will consult a well worked-out theology of suffering before we will read the passion narrative. The exact opposite is the case. The paradox is that the concrete universalizes. The fact that the gospels are compellingly concrete, telling the story of a singular man with a singular mission and a singular destiny makes rapport possible. Our suffering is able to become his; his victory is able to become ours.

The interweaving of our stories with the story of Jesus maps more clearly the journey of faith. Jesus is the forerunner, trailblazer, pioneer, pathfinder. The total event of Jesus is "what it looks like" to live within and act out of our relationship to God. The enshrined statement of this conviction is that Jesus is both God and man, divine and human. In him we contact neither God alone nor man alone but God-Man, the relationship between the divine and the human. We may make contact and be influenced by divine reality in many ways. But ultimately we look to Jesus to both affirm and critique our experiences of God and ourselves, to sharpen our sensitivities and focus our energies.

Although no one can undertake the journey of Christian faith without Jesus, we take him along in various ways. We will investigate three general orientations to Jesus—the way of admiration, the way of imitation, and the way of explanation—and more fully develop a fourth approach, the way of retelling his story.

ORIENTATIONS TO JESUS

The way of admiration focuses the gospel accounts of Jesus through a highly developed theology of the

Incarnation. The backdrop of this approach is a universal divine plan. Its classic articulation is the opening sentence of the Epistle to the Hebrews. "In times past God spoke in fragmentary and varied ways to our Fathers through the prophets; in this, the final age, he has spoken to us through his Son, whom he has made heir of all things and through whom he first created the universe." The drama of salvation begins with creation and the fall and concludes with the return of Christ, universal judgment, and everlasting damnation or bliss. At the center is the Incarnation and the Atonement. The Son of God becomes man and rescues us from our fallen condition. He has won a victory for us; and if we stay in contact with him, the benefits will be ours.

This is a classic mythic pattern. The hero journeys forth, undergoes perils but overcomes them, and returns home with the spoils. This sequence lurks behind the christological hymn of Philippians 2. The Son did not cling to the perogative of divinity but emptied himself out into human form. He became obedient unto death, even to death on a cross. "Because of this God exalted him and bestowed on him the name that is above every other name." The result of this is that our knees must bend and our mouths proclaim, "Jesus Christ is Lord." To paraphrase a liturgical response: Christ has departed, Christ has suffered, Christ has been exalted.

Our response to the Son of God who has accomplished this salvation is to praise him and give him thanks. We live in the wake of his coming and participate in the benefits of his sacrifice. It is an "admirabile commercium," a wonderful undertaking that has brought to us the boon of eternal life. From this perspective the appeal of many preachers is toward gratitude. How can our hearts remain tepid when faced with the great sacrifice of the Son of God for our well being? How can we remain ungrateful when so great a gift has been bestowed upon us? We must thank, praise and worship the incarnate Son of God.

The way of admiration marvels at the story of Jesus. Its eyes are the prologue of the Gospel of John and it sees everywhere the single, wonderful fact the prologue proclaims—the Word has become flesh. Cardinal Newman, in meditating on the birth of Jesus, talks of "omnipotence in bonds." Augustine, in relating the story of the woman at the well, focuses on the fact that Jesus is fatigued and remarks, "He who is the very strength of God is overwhelmed with lassitude." Dom Marmion, in seeking to understand how the God who created all things in a marvelous fashion did even more marvelously reform them, asks, "How could this be done? What is this Divine Marvel?" He answers, "The Mystery of the Incarnation."[3] The way of admiration is continually awe struck by God becoming man, and it rings the changes on that theme at every point in the Jesus story.

In this approach, the key moments of the Jesus story are pre-existence, birth, death, and resurrection. In fact, even the moment of resurrection is slightly anticlimatic. Once the story is started with a preexistent divine being, the fact that he will survive death and return to his home is taken for granted.

This approach then emotionally centers on birth and death and takes as its key feasts Christmas and Good Friday. In the high speculation that accompanies this approach to Jesus, the question was asked, "When did the redemption take place? At the moment the Second Person of the Blessed Trinity assumed a human nature or in his obedience to the Father through his sacrificial death?" Whether we opt with Irenaeus' incarnational emphasis and say the humanization of God is the divinization of the human or we side with Anselm's crucifixion position and say that Christ's death earned merit which he passed on to us, we are more united theologically than divided. Although the implications of each position are different, both focus on the objective fact of the redemption, its once-and-for-all quality. Although they argue passionately over the precise nature of this fact, there is a "disinterested feel," a scientific neutrality to the whole enterprise. These attempts to figure out the fact of salvation so we can pinpoint our praise more precisely highlight a serious shortcoming in the way of admiration.

The way of admiration often leads to distancing. The story of Jesus is related as a series of magnificient facts; but these are facts to be acknowledged rather than realities to be encountered. The feelings of praise, awe, and thanksgiving which these facts evoke encourage us to kneel in the presence of our Lord and bow our head in worship. But when we kneel with our heads bowed, we cannot look Jesus in the eye. With the heavy emphasis on birth and death the ministry of Jesus is often overlooked; or when it is considered, the miracles receive most of the attention. Yet it is the ministry of Jesus, his words and deeds, which affirms and critiques our words and deeds. The story of Jesus can do more than direct us to the wonder of birth and the agony of death. It can provide an entry into the struggles that characterize a faithful life. The stress on the divinity of Jesus in the way of admiration inevitably lessens our awareness of his humanity; and with a diminished humanity the possibility of actual contact, of real interaction between our life and the life story of Jesus, are reduced. To admire the Son of God who died for our sins is a genuine Christian spirituality. But it can subtly become a way of keeping at arm's length the gracious and demanding Jesus of Nazareth.

The movement from the way of admiration to the way of imitation is aptly illustrated from an incident taken from the life of Clarence Leonard Jordan. Jordan was a Baptist preacher who published the *Cotton Patch Version* of the New Testament and, in the fifties and sixties, struggled to keep alive a community in South Georgia called Koinonia Farm. The story is told that Clarence once approached his brother Robert and asked him to represent the Koinonia Farm in a legal transaction.

> "Clarence, I can't do that. You know my political aspirations. Why, if I represented you, I might lose my job, my house, everything I've got."
> "We might lose everything too, Bob."
> "It's different for you."
> "Why is it different? I remember, it seems to me, that you and I joined the church the same Sunday, as boys. I expect when we came forward the preacher asked me

about the same question he did you. He asked me, 'Do you accept Jesus as your Lord and Savior.' And I said, 'Yes' What did you say?''

"I follow Jesus, Clarence, up to a point."

"Could that point by any chance be—the cross?"

"That's right. I follow him to the cross, but not on the cross. I'm not getting myself crucified."

"Then I don't believe you're a disciple. You're an admirer of Jesus, but not a disciple of his. I think you ought to go back to the church you belong to, and tell them you're an admirer not a disciple."

"Well now, if everyone who felt like I do did that, we wouldn't have a church, would we?"

"The question," Clarence said, "is, 'Do you have a church?' "[4]

The way of imitation picks up the lack in the way of admiration. The ministry of Jesus takes precedence over his birth and death and "doing what Jesus did" is contrasted with thanking him. This approach looks at the fundamental perspectives, attitudes and actions of Jesus as models of faith responses. It hopes to find in an actual following of Jesus an orthopraxis, a salvific way to live.

The way of imitation takes place on two levels. The first level is concerned with putting on the mind and heart of Jesus. The faith that animated the life of Jesus should be the faith that animates our life. Jesus understood the Kingdom of God as the most important reality of human life and dedicated himself totally to it. Therefore we, his followers, should value beyond all else the movement of God in our lives and dedicate ourselves totally to it. Jesus was angered at the oppression of the poor by those who misused their power. We, his followers, should be angry at the oppression in our societies. James Mackey suggests that we should read Galatians 2:16 literally. "We ... who know that a man is not justified by works of the law but through the faith of Jesus Christ, even we have believed in Jesus Christ in order to be justified by the faith of Christ."[5] This passage is not urging external reliance on Jesus Christ but internal imitation of his faith. Leonardo Boff makes this type of imitation explicit. "The attitudes of Jesus ought to be followed by his disciples. They inaugurate a new type of human being and humanism, one we believe to be the most perfect that has ever emerged; and it has the capacity to assimilate new and different values without betraying its own essence."[6] This first level of imitation stresses the humanity of Jesus as similar to our own and pushes us to make the faith of Jesus our own.

The second level of imitation looks to the actual behavior of Jesus. It does not focus on his general attitudes and values but on how they are embodied in particular actions. Jesus was a man who had no place to lay his head. Therefore his followers must be poor and homeless. Jesus took a whip and drove the moneychangers from the temple. Therefore his followers must purge the church of any trafficking in money. Jesus died at the hands of the religious and political authorities of his day. There is no greater death for his followers than to be similarly martyred. The very behavior of Jesus is valid for all times and all places. Any true follower will walk in those steps.

The weakness in the way of imitation is seen most clearly when the actual behavior of Jesus is taken as a guide. The strategies which Jesus used were geared to his social, religious and political environment. Table fellowship with sinners in order to embody the faith conviction that God's grace approaches all and not just the select few was entirely appropriate to Jesus's time. Is that same strategy available to us today? Or has the changing social conditions made that particular embodiment of faith obsolete? An imitation of Jesus which tends to be slavish to the strategies he used tends also to be fundamentalistic and irrelevant to its own times. Imitation can curb creativity. In asking, "What would Jesus do?" we neglect the creative possibilities that our own ingenuity could devise. Imitation can turn to mimicry; and mimicry is the death of creative response.

The attempt to imitate the faith of Jesus is definitely on target. To make his perspectives and values our own seems to be the way of any genuine discipleship. Yet there are definite limits to this approach which the word imitation does not make clear. If Sobrino is correct,[6] the faith of Jesus developed under the pressure of the actual conflicts he was engaged in. While the basic elements of his faith remained, they were reconfigured in terms of his life history. The life history of Jesus is uniquely his own. We do not share his precise developmental pattern. Although in a general way we can participate in the perspectives of Jesus, our own life histories will purge and reconfigure those perspectives. Our actual faith, while in contact with the faith of Jesus, will have been formed, as the book of Proverbs might have put it, "in the furnace of our own fires."

Also the "inner mind" of Jesus is not available to us. What we have are "features," the general attitudes and perspectives of Jesus. In this wide sense our faith takes its orientation from the faith of Jesus. But to the degree we are introspective we are very much concerned with our own "inner mind." The moves we make within our basic faith orientation, the insights that become dominant, the values we espouse, the shifts in style and activity are uniquely our own. Looking to Jesus cannot mean not looking to ourselves. When imitation becomes mindless dependency, the Jesus who always shifted attention from himself to the movement of God which was catalyzing people into action is certainly not being followed. The remark of the Johannine Christ about the relationship of Jesus and his followers must be remembered. "I solemnly assure you, / the man who has faith in me / will do the works I do, / and greater far than these." This delicate balance between continuing the works of Jesus and enacting the "far greater" possibilities of our present situation is the essence of Christian discipleship.

The way of explanation takes a different tack from both admiration and imitation. It focuses on the person of Jesus and pursues the question of his identity. The bestowing of titles is one way to explain who Jesus Christ is. Each title—Son of God, Christ, Lord, Messiah, Son of Man, Son of David, Prophet of the Last Days—brings to light an aspect of Jesus' personality. But it should be noted that the concrete life of Jesus also reconfigures each title. The influence runs both ways. To call Jesus the Son of God tells us something about Jesus; but to call the Son of God Jesus also tells us something about the Son of God. This mutuality, this reciprocal give and take between the titles and the actual life of Jesus, keeps this approach from falling into mere flattery. Heaping titles on Jesus can be a mindless habit that distorts rather than illumines his person. The dialogue must always be maintained. The titles probe the person of Jesus; the person of Jesus probes the true meaning of the titles.

Beyond titles the way of explanation attempts to construct the inner components of Jesus' selfhood. The first five centuries of the church chronicle the vacillations of these christological constructions. The twists and turns of thought about the psychic make-up of Jesus settled into the enshrined statement of the council of Chalcedon: Jesus Christ is one person in two natures. This dogmatic formulation in turn launched centuries of more speculation. Just how are the two natures united? What are the problems of a divine and human mind and a divine and human will in the same person? Can the humanity of Jesus be adored? Why did the *Second Person* of the Trinity become man? All these questions and the more recent, scripturally oriented probe—when did Jesus know he was divine?—are attempts to detail the psychic structure of the person of Jesus.

A good example of the way of explanation is John Cobb's provocative attempt to ground the uniqueness of Jesus. He begins with the biblical data that Jesus spoke with authority. This was not simply the authority of the prophets but it was at one and the same time the authority of God. Although Jesus remained autonomous in relationship to God, at times he identified his own perceptions with those of God. The foundation for this self understanding must be the constitution of the selfhood of Jesus. The "I" of Jesus, which is the center around which experience attempts to organize itself, was constituted by the prehension (a usable synonym might be "grasping") of God in terms of that which makes him God, his love and lordship. With this mode of prehension the "I" of Jesus is uniquely composed.

> This prehension was not experienced by Jesus as information about God but as the presence of God to and in him. Furthermore, and most uniquely, it was not experienced by him as one prehension alongside others to be integrated by him into a synthesis with them. Rather this prehension of God constituted in Jesus the center from which everything else in his psychic life was integrated. This means that at least in some decisive moments of his life he perceived the world, his own past and future, his emotions and reason, in terms of the presence of God in him. At least in such moments Jesus' weighting of values—his perception of the relative importance of things and persons, of the self and others, of motives and actions, of past, present, and future—was from the perspective given in his prehension of God.[7]

Cobb attempts to explain the authority of Jesus through a process understanding of the formation of the self.

The logic of the way of explanation is exemplified in the classic formulation of Chalcedon—Jesus Christ is one person in two natures. The philosophic difficulties of this formulation are innumerable. The most prominent puzzle is how the words person and nature are being used and how they can be reconciled. But whatever the logical problems of this formulation and whatever distortions it is prone to, it is a touchstone dogma of Christian faith. As a dogma its primary role is to safeguard the experience of Jesus. In and through Jesus the truly human is touched; therefore a human nature is present. In and through Jesus the truly divine is touched; therefore a divine nature must be present. Yet this touching of humanity and divinity is not the result of encountering a schizophrenic. A truly unified person is met; therefore one person is present. This explanation of Jesus, although internally beset by problems, holds to the basic elements of any encounter with Jesus Christ.

Explanations of the person of Jesus are attempts to account for the experience of Jesus. They try to spell out the "conditions for the possibility" of a certain aspect of the encounter with Jesus. So Cobb's explanation of Jesus' oneness with God is an attempt to account for the experience of Jesus as one who spoke with authority. The fact that Jesus is considered "one in being with the Father" is because the experience of Jesus demands that type of acknowledgement. The final reason why the doctrine of the humanity and divinity of Christ is required is that it illuminates the experience of Jesus. "It is the precise nature of the faith he [Jesus] enabled them to have which dictates the precise nature of the acknowledgement required of them."[8] The way of explanation is a secondary procedure. It is the reflective process people engage in after they have encountered Jesus and through him have experienced the salvation of God.

When contemporary christologies focus on the person of Jesus, they are presupposing that he is important. His person is worthy of speculative exploration. He has had such an impact on people that the ancient gospel question, "Who do men say that I am?" is alive and well today. But if people have not experienced salvation through Jesus of Nazareth, his identity is of little importance. This is the primacy of the relational. Without salvific contact who cares? Unless Jesus has touched and transformed and continues to touch and transform personal lives, speculation about him or his possible influence is gratuitous. To ask what is the meaning of Jesus for world history, political structures or interpersonal living assumes that he is so significant that what he did and said should have an impact on those areas. But where does this conviction of importance come from? It must come from an encounter of such depth and power that it is natural to try to extend its influence to all aspects of life. The bedrock of all christology is that in the presence of Jesus we are the people of God.

From what we know of the historical Jesus he focused neither on himself nor on God. The central motif of his preaching and his life was the Kingdom of God, the movement of people in God and the movement of God in people. Jesus activated this movement. When Jesus was with people, the God who was previously dormant was awake and active. When Jesus moved out of their lives, God quieted down. When Jesus returned, God stirred. Out of this experience—that the presence of Jesus meant the presence of God—they then asked the question, "Who could this person be?" When we are with him, we are touched and transformed by all that is Holy. When he goes away, the Holy also recedes. He must have a special relationship to God because when we are with him, we have a special relationship to God.

The primacy of the relational means that our language about Jesus, like our language about God, cuts both ways. There is always a self-referent in Jesus-talk. To say Jesus is compassionate is not, in the first moment, to posit the quality of compassion in the soul of Jesus; but it is to say, "When I am with Jesus, I experience him experiencing me from the inside." To say Jesus is loving is not, in the first moment, to posit the quality of love in the heart of Jesus; but it is to say, "When I am with Jesus, I experience myself as being loved." When people do not experience God through Jesus, christology becomes a hangover, a habit inherited from previous generations who did experience God through Jesus.

The only reason to admire Jesus is if when we have contacted him, there is much that is admirable. The only reason to imitate Jesus is if when we have encountered him, his life is so appealing and attractive that we wish to link our lives most closely to it. The only reason to deeply explore the person of Jesus is because through that person we have experienced the depth of our own personhood. Everything hinges on contact with him and transformation through him. In other words, is his presence the entry into the movement of God which is ultimately gracious and salvific? If it is, then we must focus on him and through him on ourselves. If it is not, he is dispensable.

This is a hard test. But not one the Jesus of the gospels would shrink from. When the Baptist was in prison, he sent his disciples to inquire about Jesus. "Are you the One who is to come or should we look for another?" Jesus' response is to ask them, "What do you see?" And then, in an uncharacteristic way, he answers his own question, quoting from Isaiah: "The blind recover their sight, cripples walk, lepers are cured, the deaf hear, dead men are raised to life, and the poor have the good news preached to them." This is an empirical answer. "I am the one because what is destructive is giving way to what is creative." Jesus does not say, "Yes, I am the One!" and proudly rest on that statement. He does not presume any authority independent of his impact. Even John has him say, "If you cannot believe in me, believe in the works I do." Jesus is the one because he makes things happen. Contact with him is the transformation of life. This concrete criterion, favored by Jesus as the way to know if he was important, is no different today.

It should be noted this is not a question of did people experience salvation through Jesus of Nazareth. Even the most skeptical historian would have to answer that affirmatively. The gospels and the whole of Christian history witness to the fact that Jesus mediated the power of the sacred. The question is: does Jesus mediate salvation today? What we are pursuing is an encounter with Jesus of Nazareth. The faith that comes from only hearing *about* Jesus is not enough. In the gospel of John, after

Andrew has talked to Jesus and experienced life through him, he runs to his brother Simon to tell him that he has found the Messiah. Simon does not take it on Andrew's word but goes out to meet Jesus. The result is one of the most fascinating relationships in scripture, the tumultuous interaction between the impetuous Peter and the masterful Jesus. The only response to someone else's experience of God through Jesus is to see if that experience is available to us through Jesus. To pick up a theme of the last chapter, we live in an age where inherited beliefs are becoming personalized beliefs or they are being abandoned. We are in the position of the Samaritans who first believed because the woman at the well told them about Jesus, but later believed because they had met Jesus. While revering our tradition, we must be able to say to it: "No longer does our faith depend on your story. We have heard for ourselves, and we know that this really is the Savior of the world."

Two established ways of contacting Jesus Christ are through the lives of the saints and the cultic mysteries. Like all religious traditions, Christianity has its holy people. In well ordered times objective criteria of holiness are established. If a person prays and fasts, performs acts of penance and charity, he or she is considered to be holy. Yet existential holiness cannot be determined by behavioral norms. In the presence of certain people we are catapulted into the presence of God. We call these people holy because through them we are initiated into holiness. Their presence activates the presence of God. Yet these people, in turn, talk about the fact that they experience God through Jesus. They see themselves as the followers of Christ and very often attribute any good that comes from their lives to Jesus Christ. As Chesterton remarked about Francis of Assisi: if we say that Francis of Assisi is something like Christ, we must also say that Christ was something like Francis of Assisi. Therefore, we contact Jesus Christ in a mediated fashion through those people who take up and exemplify his life in a particular way. But, of course, this only pushes the question back one step. How did the saints get to know Jesus Christ? How did Francis of Assisi encounter Jesus?

The most enshrined way of contacting Jesus Christ is not to focus on the Jesus but to explore the Christ. The central doctrine of Christianity is that Jesus of Nazareth is the Risen Lord. As the Risen Lord, he is no longer bound to time and space. In fact he permeates all time and all space; and so contact with the resurrected Christ can occur at any time or at any place. The Christ of the apocryphal gospel of Thomas says: "I am the light which is above all things. I am the universe. The universe parted from me and the universe returned to me. Cut open a piece of firewood and I am there within. Raise up a stone and I am underneath it." The answer to where can we find Christ today is simply everywhere.

Within the ubiquitous presence of the resurrected Christ the eucharistic liturgy has special access to him. There have been many theories of the real presence of Christ. Some have focused directly on the bread and wine; others have looked to the total eucharistic action. But it is always a question of whether the theories have fully accounted for the adamant article of faith—Christ is really present. Perhaps the tradition's strongest statement is that Christ is present "ex opere operato." His presence is assured independently of the holiness of the priest or the people participating. In more updated language the eucharist is called "a guaranteed encounter" with the Risen Lord. For our purposes, all eucharistic theory is an attempt to spell out the way in which we make contact. The bottom line is that there is a locale and action which gives direct access to the Resurrected Christ. To encounter Jesus Christ it seems we have to go no farther than the local church on a Sunday morning.

Yet this language of "encountering the Risen Lord," whether in the liturgy or elsewhere, is slippery. It tends to be used within the supernaturalistic imagination and creates a difficulty that is the reverse of picturing God as an Invisible Supreme Being. The reality of God is everywhere. When the imagination unwittingly pictures an invisible divine body, the presence is restricted to the proportions of that body. The highly accessible God is rendered highly inaccessible. With the reality of Jesus Christ the problem is the same, only turned around. The phrases Resurrected Christ and Risen Lord cannot avoid pointing to the continued yet transformed presence of Jesus of Nazareth. Unless there is to be a total discontinuity between the historical Jesus and the Resurrected Christ, it is necessary to continue to link the Risen Lord with Jesus the Jew. But when the imagination sees Christ everywhere, this link is subtly broken. The Risen Lord becomes a free-floating divine presence disassociated from the historical Jesus who cannot float free. Christ is a totally available reality. All we need do is turn our minds and hearts to him. An intentional act makes immediate contact. But what is contacted has no "density" or "thickness." Since our imaginations have left behind the flesh and blood contours of this historical Jesus, encountering the Risen Lord comes dangerously close to a ghostly meeting. The supernaturalistic imagination tied God down when the reality demanded release; now it releases the Risen Lord when the reality demands it be tied down to the historical Jesus. Jon Sobrino points to this problem in his analysis of the dysfunctions of cult in Christian history.

> ... the gradual cultualization of Christian faith was due to a specific conception of the Risen Christ. Since he was the Lord, it was possible to establish a relationship with him in the present; more and more cultic worship came to be regarded as the locale where that relationship was established. Once that happened, cultic worship could take predominance in Christianity over every other aspect of Christian living—specifically, over the concrete obligation of discipleship.[9]

Direct contact with the Risen Lord does not seem to be as complex and demanding as face-offs with Jesus of Nazareth.

Bonding Christ to Jesus does not restrict the meaning of the resurrection to the validation of the life of Jesus of Nazareth. The resurrection is an experience in itself and opens up new vistas and new dimensions of reality. It is a wondrous expression of God's justice and fidelity and infinitely expands the destiny of Jesus. But wherever the Risen Lord goes, he carries the memory of the historical Jesus. It is this man who is professed as the Resurrected Christ. Therefore, the record of his life must be a clue to why he, as opposed to so many others, is professed as the Son of God. Over the centuries Christian artists have placed Jesus in the highest heaven, at the right hand of the Father and surrounded by angels and saints; but he always has holes in his hands. The connection between the historical life of Jesus and the risen life of Jesus Christ must be firmly held.

The question remains: Can we today experience salvation through Jesus of Nazareth? Perhaps. We have the stories, the stories Jesus told and the stories people told about him. They are written down in the our gospels. But those pages cannot contain them. They move into the mouths and ears of people where they are much more at home. We retell and rehear the stories. There is a possibility that in the retelling and rehearing we will enter our relationship to Mystery in a new and transformed way. We might touch God afresh. If we do, we will praise and imitate and explore the person whose recorded memory was so gracious to us. This way of contacting Jesus— retelling his stories and those about him—is built on a trinitarian understanding of God. Without a fully appropriated trinitarian perspective Jesus of Nazareth sinks into the sea of the past.

It is often said that the Trinity is the most distinctive Christian dogma. The belief that God is triune sets off Christianity from other religions. Yet the Trinity also has the popular reputation of being the most speculative and abstract of doctrines. It is professed as part of the revered tradition but its existential meaning is seldom understood. If the "in" accusation of a few years back was that Christians were crypto-Monophysites (people who allow the divine nature of Christ to swallow the human nature), today the charge might be crypto-Unitarians, verbalizing a triune God but thinking and acting from a unitarian perspective. Yet the doctrine of the Trinity is not a flight of fancy or a needless complication of the simplicity of God. It is a formulation which reflects the peculiar Christian history of experiencing the movement of God in human life.

The trinitarian experience of God is grounded in the fact that Jesus leaves twice. First, he departs into the realm of death from which he emerges triumphant. Secondly, he departs for his permanent home with God. Whatever else the ascension narrative may convey, it is undoubtedly a picture of departure. The inescapable message is that Jesus is no longer available in the way he once was. In his absence the stories he told and the story he was are remembered and retold by his followers. The meal which was a sign of his ministry is reenacted in memory of past fellowship and in hope of his return to establish a new fellowship. Reginald Fuller characterizes the earliest Christology as a two-pole perspective—Jesus' earthly life and his return to inaugurate the end time.[10] But it should be noted that the people who had this perspective were standing in the middle of Jesus' absence.

With the delay of the parousia the two-pole, horizontal Christology turned into a two-stage, vertical understanding of the destiny of Jesus—Jesus' earthly life and his role as Lord and Christ sitting at the right hand of the Father and sending the Spirit to the church. As time took the early church farther away from the earthly Jesus yet no nearer to Jesus as the returning Son of Man, the emphasis on the experience of the Spirit increased. In fact, many argue that for Paul and the Pauline communities there is a functional identity between the Spirit and the Risen Lord.

> For, like Paul, they mainly experience and understand the resurrection of Jesus as the gift of the Spirit, and the missionary activity which ensued from this, as new life, the experience of forgiveness and the act of changing one's ways known as repentence, as new faith, and as eucharistic presence.[11]

The proclaimed experience of the resurrection of Jesus translates into the experience of Jesus as an "exalted power or spirit"[12] in the lives of his followers. This is not a denial of Jesus' personal destiny with God but a simultaneous conviction of the absence of Jesus in one way and his presence in another. It seems that Jesus is available to be encountered but only through the Spirit of God.

The experience which Jesus was able to trigger did not go into the far reaches of God with him. What happened when the earthly Jesus was with people continued to happen when the earthly Jesus was not with them. Yet this experience of God was so linked to the person of Jesus that it was inconceivable to experience God as Father without simultaneously experiencing the Son who bodied him forth. The logic was inescapable. The God of Jesus was here, so Jesus must be here. But Jesus is definitely not here as he once was. Rather his Spirit is present among us. And since the Spirit belongs to Jesus and the Father, it is capable of initiating an experience of God as Father through Jesus as Son.

How do we contact the Jesus who now lives in the immensity of God? The answer is through the reality that both we and Jesus share—the reality of God. A strange reversal has taken place. It is the switch that distinguishes the first disciples of Jesus from all who come after. The people who met Jesus, in the stately phrase of faith, "in the days of his flesh" contacted God through him. The people of later times contact Jesus through God in the person of the Spirit. In the times of Jesus God was missing (what John Bowker calls the problem of "theistic effect")[13] and Jesus was available. In the times after Jesus the Spirit of God is now available and Jesus is missing. At one time the present Jesus became an encounter with the absent God. At another time the now present Spirit of God becomes a way of encountering the absent Jesus. Paul says the Spirit in us cries, "Abba." But that is Jesus' word. The Spirit cries, "Jesus," the gift remembers the giver. The giver cries, "Father;" and together all cry our name.

There is a medieval dictum that enshrines the trinitarian experience of God: "Opera trinitatas ad extra sunt indivisa" (the work of the Trinity among creatures is all of one piece). In other words, Christians have a permanent threefold relationship to God. We dwell now with the Spirit who is actively at work soliciting our freedom and transforming our lives and our environments. But this Spirit directs our mind and hearts to the events of which Jesus is the center. Jesus is the Son, the concrete embodiment of God; and any experience of the divine gravitates toward him. Yet the Son carries our minds and hearts to the ultimate reaches of the transcendent Mystery we live within and calls it Father—generating love. Often the trinitarian structure of our relationship to the mystery of God is expressed as belief in the Father *and* Son *and* the Holy Spirit. But this conjunctional approach misses the dynamism of the experience. The prepositions are important. We live *in* the Spirit and go *through* the Son *to* the Father.

The preposition "through" is key to the experience of Jesus. Jesus is not stopped at or stared at; he is gone through. This returns us to the metaphor of journey and expands it. The journey of faith is begun when we move out of our conviction of ultimate graciousness into the fray of everyday living. It is at this point that the clarity of faith becomes murky and the serenity of faith becomes conflictual. Our thoughts freeze, our feelings become nebulous, and our actions turn half-hearted. But the story of Jesus is the story of faith in the concrete. He is the visibility of the invisible movement of God; and contact with him means the specification of God's intention and the spark to go on. To experience Jesus is to experience yourself "on track," in the Spirit and on the way to the Father. This trinitarian approach is the inevitable structure of every meeting with Jesus after his death, resurrection, and ascension.

In their basic format the four gospels reflect this quality of any encounter with Jesus. The evangelists were not neutral collectors and arrangers of the Jesus material. They had points to make and Jesus was one of the ways they made them. To some extent the Jesus who emerges in each gospel carries the theological agenda of the writer. Therefore it is necessary to talk about a Matthean, Markan, Lukan, and Johannine Christ. This is not an indiscriminate manipulation of the Jesus data. Rather it is a creative retelling so certain emphases in the life and message of Jesus address the present situation of the community.

This liberty with the received Jesus tradition often strikes us as inappropriate. With our "Woodward and Bernstein" approach, exact names, dates and words are highly prized. But for the evangelists Jesus can be understood in three ways—as a past historical figure, as the living Lord at the right hand of the Father, and as a presence among them through his Spirit. Therefore, they structure the remembered elements of his earthly story so that his continued presence in the Spirit can be discerned. The Spirit of Jesus is at work in the community but its intentions are difficult to discern. The story of the Giver of the Spirit clarifies the Spirit's urgings and maps the journey to the Father.

The gospels of Mark and Luke form a good contrast and bring out this function of the overall Jesus story. For the persecuted yet hopeful community of Mark, Jesus is the suffering Son of Man who will return to judge the living and the dead. But for the community of Luke which is settling down in history, this end-time portrait is modified. Jesus becomes the exemplar of Christian life. Like the believer, Jesus prays and attends worship: like Jesus, the believer forgives his executioners (Stephen). Differing historical and religious conditions provoke different renditions of Jesus. Certain features of the story become prominent because they speak to a given situation. These features in turn organize and reinterpret the rest of the tradition. The evangelists constructed the gospels so that Jesus would be meaningful to the present situation of the community. This was not a faddish attempt at relevance. Under the influence of life in the Spirit and on the way to the Father, they were sensitive to certain dimensions of the personal and written memory of Jesus. They retold the story of the Son so that the path to the Father was revealed and the movement of the Spirit clarified.

Today this trinitarian approach to Jesus (which is the only consistent approach possible) takes its own specific form. The quest for the historical Jesus or, to keep the phrasing as accurate as possible, that portrait of Jesus which current historical methods would consider reliable, is the dominant approach to the gospels. This approach is often accused of pandering to the times, or overlooking the heart of Christian faith which is the divinity of Christ, or reducing Jesus to what at the moment the modern world is capable of affirming. But from a trinitarian perspective an alternate understanding is possible. Under the impact of the Spirit people are deeply exploring their commonly shared humanity, specifically in terms of its historical development. The way to the Father is not to escape the conditions of individual and social living but to transform them. If these broadly sketched emphases are how the immanent and transcendent Mystery of God is being experienced, the humanity and historicity of Jesus will be pursued so that we can enter our own humanity and historicity through his. So the gospels, which are complex blends of history and myth, are prosecuted so that a portrait of the historical humanity of Jesus emerges. The quest for the historical Jesus is not a matter of mere fascination ("What was he really like?"), or a desire to be critically and rationally precise ("Sorry, old boy. He never said that. Fabrication of John, you know.") but the most recent expression of Christian trinitarian instincts, moving out of the Spirit through the Son to the Father.

Under the influence of the contemporary concern for history and humanity the wholistic gospels are divided into the Jesus of history and the Christ of faith. In the portrait of the historical Jesus interpretation is kept at a minimum. The profile is an attempt to describe the pre-Easter Jesus, as untouched as possible by the theological elaborations which flow from the resurrection experience. In the past, reconstructions of the historical Jesus have been notoriously conflicting and so tied to the current cultural mood that the face of Jesus looked remarkably like the face of the investigating historian. Today, however, there is a new scholarly confidence that a consensus which is historically responsible can be achieved. Norman Perrin's summary reflects the main themes of this consensus and his last line conveys the new attitude of confidence and sufficiency.

> He was baptized by John the Baptist, and the beginning of his ministry was in some way linked with that of the Baptist. In his own ministry Jesus was above all the one who proclaimed the Kingdom of God and who challenged his hearers to respond to the reality he was proclaiming. The authority and effectiveness of Jesus as proclaimer of the Kingdom of God was reinforced by an apparently deserved reputation as an exorcist. In a world that

believed in gods, in powers of good and evil, and in demons, he was able, in the name of God and his Kingdom, to help those who believed themselves to be possessed by demons.

A fundamental concern of Jesus was to bring together into a unified group those who responded to his proclamation of the Kingdom of God irrespective of their sex, previous background or history. A central feature of the life of this group was eating together, sharing a common meal that celebrated their unity in the new relationship with God, which they enjoyed on the basis of their response to Jesus' proclamation of the Kingdom. In this concern for the unity of the group of those who responded to the proclamation, Jesus challenged the tendency of the Jewish community of his day to fragment itself and in the name of God to reject certain of its own members. This aroused a deep-rooted opposition to him, which reached a climax during a Passover celebration in Jerusalem when he was arrested, tried by the Jewish authorities on a charge of blasphemy and by the Romans on a charge of sedition, and crucified. During his lifetime he had chosen from among his followers a small group of disciples who had exhibited in their work in his name something of his power and authority.

That, or something very like it, is all that we can know; it is enough.[14]

It should be kept in mind that the historical Jesus is an interpreted portrait. On one level, all we have available of Jesus' life and sayings is what was remembered and recorded by the early church. This memory was not neutral but highly selective. On a second level, the very method of historiography introduces critical interpretive principles. The portrait of the historical Jesus is not a theory-free picture. But it is an interpretation with objectivity as its guiding value.

The Forerunner of Faith

The Christ of faith is a portrait of Jesus heavily influenced by the resurrection experience of the early church. It is an interpretation of Jesus that has the inner meaning of his impact as its guiding value. Although the portrait of the historical Jesus is the result of both the interaction of the early church with the actual Jesus and the interaction of the historian with the materials of the gospels, the role of the early church and historian are kept in the background. In the portrait of the Christ of faith the role of those who contact Jesus is in the foreground. What happened to them in their interaction with Jesus is the main concern of the stories they tell. To call Jesus the Lamb and the Vine is not to engage in historical reconstruction. These are metaphors of significance. They carry acknowledgement and allegiance. To tell a story of Peter sinking in the waves till Jesus' hand steadies him is not a piece of historical reporting. It is a story conveying Christ's saving power for the life of the early church. The portrait of the Christ of faith openly and unashamedly rises from the relationship of Jesus Christ and the early church. It is a technicolor picture of his impact.

Therefore, the possibility exists today of inhabiting the gospels from the point of view of the portrait of the historical Jesus *and* the portrait of the Christ of faith. There is a definite continuity in these portraits. Dermot Lane remarks that the resurrection which is the trigger for the faith portrait "must never be seen as something which imposes a meaning on the life of Jesus from the outside as if it were some *coup de force*. Rather the resurrection clarifies what is already imminent in

155

the words and deeds of Jesus.''[15] However, it is the portrait of the historical Jesus which is most fascinating. Today, to say "the historical Jesus is the Christ of faith" is more than a statement of gospel continuity. It enshrines a contemporary preference. People take their lives to this historical Jesus for affirmation and challenge.

Faith in Jesus is a process of relating our own lives to his life story. It is a procedure of going through him into the Spirit and onto the Father. As faith in God entailed an inner process of handing life over and receiving it back, so faith in Jesus entails a process of handing power over to his story and receiving it back into our own. We allow the life story of Jesus to focus the areas of importance in human life and to give a perspective on those areas. In no way do we give up our critical faculties but we allow the story to guide and sharpen their use. The story of Jesus which is the initial partner in this dialogue is the historical portrait. The Jesus of history is the Christ of faith for today because it is to him that we come with our lives.

Two important considerations flow from this basic starting point. The first concerns the portrait of the Christ of faith in the gospels. The emphasis on the portrait of the historical Jesus is not meant to exclude the beautiful stories and brilliant theologies of the more explicit faith picture. They carry the intention of truth and are indispensable to our contact with the life, death and resurrection of Jesus. To start with the historical portrait is merely to inhabit and appreciate the fully developed faith statements in a distinctive way. A few quotes from contemporary studies of Jesus will point up the proper relationship between the two portraits.

> Historical or not, the story of Jesus' entry into Jerusalem riding on a donkey is typical; not the victor's white horse, not an animal symbolizing dominion, but the mount used by the poor and powerless.[16]

> Whatever historians may say about the stable at Bethlehem, as a symbol it is absolutely to the point.[17]

> 'Not my will but your will be done.' Even if this is not a *verbum ipsissimum*, not a historical Jesus-saying, it unmistakably reflects the inner consistency of Jesus' own preaching and personal bearing during his life.[18]

Whatever historical judgments may be made on the donkey, the stable and the garden surrender, the truth of the impact of Jesus is expressed in these symbols and hopefully communicated to generations of Christians.

Although the portrait of the Christ of faith adds color and commitment to the starker lines of the historical sketch, it cannot be our starting point. The Christ of faith is a picture of a redemptive encounter with Jesus. Yet it is just this redemptive encounter that we are looking for. The faith portrait is about the business of expressing what it has found. We are about the business of finding something to express. Also a good deal of the faith portrait is the mere proclamation of importance. To call Jesus the Word, as the prologue to the gospel of John does, is to anchor him in the established imagery and philosophy of both Jewish and Hellenistic cultures and extend his meaning indefinitely. Jesus is now connected with the Word of God which created all things and with the principle of reason which is present throughout all reality. This tells us he is significant but it does not tell us why he is significant. It is not enough to answer that God raised him from the dead and therefore he must be important. This just moves the question back a step.

What was it about Jesus of Nazareth that was so significant that God raised him from the dead? The suggestion of Christian generations is that it was through Jesus that God was reconciling the world to himself. People who contacted him felt the power of this reconcilation. This is the experience the faith portrait presupposes and to which the titles and stories of faith refer. This is also the experience we seek.

If we do experience salvation through Jesus of Nazareth, a second consideration comes into play. If in our contact with the historical portrait of Jesus the journey of God in the Spirit and to the Father is activated, we will call Jesus the Son, the Lord, the Christ, the Logos, the Unbegotten One. In other words, we will engage ourselves in the same process as the first followers of Jesus. Our contact with divine reality through the story of Jesus will erupt in images and stories. We will connect him with all we know, for through him all we encounter has been illumined in a new way. The images, stories, and theologies of the New Testament remain our touchstones and our guides. We will own them from the inside and to them we will add our own. We are now no longer merely the inheritors of the tradition but its perpetuators. We may say Jesus is Lord not because someone told us that in him God has entered some vague reality called human existence; but because through him God has touched the concrete reality of our human existence.

W. H. Auden has written that when grace enters there is no choice, humans must dance. The faith portrait of Christ in the gospels and our own portrait of faith is dancing in response to the grace initiated by Jesus. The images, stories and theologies surrounding Jesus are not a carefully manipulated campaign to insure him a special hearing. They are the overflow of God's presence through him. They are the wild and brilliant things people do and say when the bounded love of God has been unleashed in their lives. If in taking our lives to the historical portrait of Jesus the Spirit we dwell in stirs and the Father we move towards speaks, we will inhabit the received portrait of the Christ of faith and embellish it with our own images. We do not do this out of obligation or protocol; but because we have experienced salvation through Jesus and this is what is instinctively done.

Before we consider some examples of retelling the story of Jesus, it would be helpful to retrace our steps. The ways of admiration, imitation, and explanation presuppose some experience of Jesus that would lead to praise, the adoption of his perspectives, attitudes and life style, and interest in his person. Contact with the saints of Jesus and direct access to the Risen Lord, especially in cultic worship, only push us back to the recorded memory of Jesus in the gospels. But this memory can only move beyond information and become a contemporary experience from a trinitarian perspective. Living in the Spirit and on the way to the Father we look to the Son. We allow him to show us the path of the journey. We do this by retelling the stories he told and the stories told about him so that the direction of the Spirit in our lives is clarified. Today the Spirit initially directs our attention to our historical humanity. Therefore, we approach the recorded memory of Jesus with the concerns of historical development and human transformation and well-being. The result is that we inhabit the holistic gospel portrait through the distinction of the Jesus of history and the Christ of faith. It is through the portrait of the historical Jesus, his concerns and conflicts, that the strivings of the Spirit in our history and humanity will be named and called forth. And it is through this experience that we will both appropriate the portrait of the Christ of faith in the gospels and supplement that portrait with our own expressions of what we have found through Jesus of Nazareth.

Faith in Jesus means retelling the Jesus stories so that the life of the teller is interwoven with the tale. The core of the process is the interaction of two stories—the life story of the individual and the inherited story of Jesus. Of course, the initial story interaction leads to insights, values, implications, and decisions. But as the last chapter pointed out, it is the story exchange which initiates the process and which is continually returned to in the course of the conversation. A few examples will concretize this way of resorting to Jesus.

Five couples meet once every two months. The

purpose of the gathering is to talk about what it means to be a Christian. They all share a common insight and desire. The church should be more than a social club but it (bishops and priests) should not be a moral nag telling everybody what to do. The exercise for this particular evening is to retrieve either a story about Jesus or a story Jesus told which "speaks to them."

One of the men, Tom, says he has no trouble in picking out his favorite. It is the story of the woman caught in adultery. The leader asks him to tell the group the story. He proceeds in general agreement with the Johannine rendition until he gets to Jesus' own words.

> And then Jesus said, "Let him who is without sin cast the first stone." Which means—"If anyone here has not at one time or another screwed up, or hurt, or even destroyed people close to himself let him cast the first stone." What fascinates me is the way Jesus was always his own man. Everyone else has a rock in his hand and Jesus does not. Why? He does not accept everyday judgments. He tries to think and feel what is most true in the situation. That's important.

From this beginning the group beings to talk about the problems of "being yourself." Other stories of Jesus, personal life stories, and episodes from other peoples lives are brought into the conversation.

In terms of our discussion, Tom is living in the Spirit and on the way to the Father. Like all journeys this one has conflicts and questions, demands courage and support. Yet, for Tom, the conflicts are specified in the interaction between his life history and the story of the woman taken in adultery. He must have personal integrity and not give in to mass stonings. In the course of the evening Tom relates how he has tried to deal with this struggle which he thinks is central to human living. He talks in terms of being compassionate, always giving a fair hearing, not jumping to conclusions. The initial story match-up has given way to insights, implications, and finally to stories of enacted faith. He tells about a few times when he tried to let the value of compassion guide him. Sometimes he felt he bettered the situation; other times he felt it made no difference.

The story of the woman taken in adultery would probably not qualify as reliable historical material. It is part of the portrait of the Christ of faith. But it is a story which has many of the concerns of the historical portrait in it. What Tom takes from it, how he retells it, is not the only meaning the story can generate; but it is a meaning that speaks to Tom and it is an area of life which the historical Jesus struggled with. The question of remaining faithful to "a vision which is truest" and allowing it to guide your actions is a theme in the portrait of the historical Jesus. To this extent Tom has picked up the historical core present in the story and allowed it to focus and inform his own struggle.

One of the things that characterizes pastoral settings is open-endedness. The way the stories of Jesus are retold and what is drawn from them is startling and unpredictable. There is not the control on the conversation that academic concerns impose. The gospels are being used religiously. The stories are told by people on the journey about the pioneer who blazed the trail. What is important is that the path is traveled, that the fundamental conflicts, concerns and attitudes of Jesus are passed on. The burning question is: What are these people going to do with this concern of life? Will they continue to struggle with it and handle it in a way that is in fundamental conformity to Christian values and perspectives? The story of Jesus has focused the question and given them a perspective. It has sparked the ecclesial process of people thinking and feeling and acting in the Spirit through the stories of the Son on the way to the transcendent end of all life, the love of God the Father.

A second example concerns an older woman and a "far out" connection which led to a rich discussion and some radically changed perspectives. The leader read the story of the unmerciful servant. The king had forgiven the servant nine million dollars but he turned around and throttled a fellow servant who owed him a mere fifteen dollars. The response of an older woman in the group was immediate. "I know why the servant treated the other servant so badly. He really hated being forgiven the debt by the king. So he worked out his hatred on his fellow servant." There are no indications in the scripture story that this was the servant's motive. If there is always an interplay between the Jesus stories and our own life stories, this time the personal input is extremely strong. Yet the story does deal with forgiveness; and forgiveness is a major theme in the portrait of the historical Jesus. So the story has done its initial work. It has placed the person and the group in an area of life that the historical portrait of Jesus considered important and has provided an initial perspective on that area. The group which lives in the Spirit and is on the way to the Father now concerns itself with the reality of forgiveness for that journey.

A third example of relating personal life stories to the Jesus stories is found in Mary Gordon's novel *Final Payments.* Isabel Moore had stayed home and cared for her sick father for eleven years. When he finally died, she ventured into the outside world only to be shocked and frightened by her feelings of love for a married man. She retreats to the home of her former housekeeper (Margaret) whom she has always hated and at one time kept from marrying her father. Margaret is a pathetic and spiteful woman. After the elderly Fr. Mulcahy visits Isabel, Margaret vaguely accuses them of sexual conduct. "He's capable of anything when he's had too much to drink." In a rage Isabel breaks two glasses. Margaret says she will have to pay for them because "I am a poor woman." Isabel shouts "The poor you have always with you," and storms upstairs.

> It is one of the marvels of a Catholic education that the impulse of a few words can bring whole narratives to light with an immediacy and a clarity that are utterly absorbing. "The poor you have always with you." I knew where Christ had said that: at the house of Martha and Mary. Mary had opened a jar of ointment over Christ's feet. Spikenard, I remembered. And she wiped his feet with her hair. Judas had rebuked her: he had said that the ointment ought to be sold for the poor. But, St. John had noted, Judas had said that only because he kept the purse and was a thief. And Christ had said to Judas, Mary at his feet, her hair spread out around him, "The poor you have always with you: but me you have not always."

And until that moment, climbing the dark stairs in a rage to my ugly room, it was a passage I had not understood. It seemed to justify to me the excesses of centuries of fat, tyrannical bankers. But now I understood. What Christ was saying, what he meant, was that the pleasures of that hair, that ointment, must be taken. Because the accidents of death would deprive us soon enough. We must not deprive ourselves, our loved ones, of the luxury of our extravagant affections. We must not try to second-guess death by refusing to love the ones we loved in favor of the anonymous poor.

And it came to me, fumbling in the hallway for the light, that I had been a thief. Like Judas, I had wanted to hide gold, to count it in the dead of night, to parlay it into some safe and murderous investment. It was Margaret's poverty I wanted to steal, the safety of her inability to inspire love. So that never again would I be found weeping, like Mary, at the tombstone at the break of dawn. . . .

I knew now I must open the jar of ointment. I must open my life. I knew now that I must leave. But I was not ready. I would have to build my strength.[19]

The question that immediately comes to mind is: Is all that in the story of Jesus, Mary, and Judas? The only answer is: Yes, when it is remembered by Isabel Moore at this particular time in her life. The story allows her to enter her fear of risking herself and being hurt in a new way; and it pushes her toward a fundamental trust that encourages her to love in spite of the inevitability of loss. Even if the episode is not in itself historically reliable, it reflects the concerns of the historical Jesus and the struggle the Spirit is initiating in Isabel. In many ways it was the Catholic culture which provided Isabel with the temptation to run from life. Yet it was, among other things, the Jesus story that forced her back into it.

Did Tom, the older woman and Isabel Moore experience salvation through Jesus of Nazareth? That would be for them to say. But what seems undeniable is that they entered into their own lives with questions and conflicts which the story of Jesus focused in a particular way. To have faith in Jesus is to allow the story to have some sway in our lives. It is to resort to the story, to engage in the dialogue, to hand power over and receive it back. It is to retell the story so that the teller is told.

The following chapters provide three retellings of the Jesus story. They have the historical concerns of Jesus at their heart; but they freely use the inherited imagery of the Christ of faith portrait and contemporary imagery and stories which arise from contact with the historical portrait. They are not meant to be taken in themselves, but as part of the storytelling process outlined in chapter three. They do not attempt a well-rounded portrait of either Jesus or his most current band of followers, but are highly selective in insight and imagery. They are not meant to substitute for the gospel constructions which inspired them, but to be a retelling in the light of *some* contemporary experiences. It is difficult to maintain the Christian fact unless it has diverse embodiments in a Christian culture. These stories are one of the ways the followers of Jesus respond to him and one of the ways the Christian culture is built up.

The first story, *The Indiscriminate Host*, focuses on the meal ministry of Jesus and the experience of God which is possible through the symbolism of eating and drinking. The second story, *The Son Who*

Must Die, considers the vocational struggle of Jesus and the themes of power and sacrifice. The third story, *The Storyteller of God,* takes a clue from Hans Kung's remark: "Jesus could perhaps be described as a public storyteller of the kind that can be seen even today addressing hundreds of people in the main square of an Eastern city."[20] When the Jesus stories are retold in the mouths of Christians and reheard in their ears, they are stories of faith. More than historical interest in the founder is at work. They are bringing together the lives of the followers and the life of the master and allowing the two to flow into one another.

In the last analysis these three stories, and the countless other stories which Christians tell today, are passed around because one of William Faulkner's characters was wrong, even if beautifully so, when he said:

> . . . language . . . that meager and fragile thread by which the little surface corners and edges of men's secret and solitary lives may be joined for an instant now and then before sinking back into the darkness where the spirit cried for the first time and was not heard and will cry for the last time and will not be heard either.[21]

Stories do bind the corners of our lives together but not in a doomed effort. When the spirit cried the first time, it was heard by Jesus; and when it will cry the last time, it will be heard by Jesus and us.

Chapter Five

The Indiscriminate Host

One day
Jesus looked up,
not to the drunken sky
lurching and weaving on its way,
dazzling and darkening all beneath it,
but to the late afternoon crowd
rumbling lunchless toward him,
hungry for more than God's word.
    "Where will we find enough food?"
The eternal worry of the host.
But the bread he broke defied arithmetic,
multiplying while it divided;
and the blessed fish spawned baskets of brothers.
Afterwards, John says, the crowd
belched up a crown and forged
from their fullness a scepter.
But Jesus fled to the mountain alone
to council in the court of the only King.

Another day
The Monitors of the Stomachs of the Poor
rolled a question to the smoothness of a river rock
and flung it at Jesus.
    "Why do not your disciples fast?"
To the question of fast
came the question of feast.

The Indiscriminate Host

"How can they fast
when the Bridegroom is with them?"
The logic of spite
is the snap of a snake.
"Ah! Now we know.
You are a drunkard and a glutton!"

Jesus said:
"You are like the children in the marketplace
who try to play the day away.
One pipes a festive marriage tune;
the others whine, 'We do not want to dance.'
So from his horn he drags a dirge;
the others whine, 'We do not want to mourn.'
Now John came
like a long suppressed rage
with the news the ax was at the roots
and fire awaits the fruitless.
And you said,
'The grasshopper eater chews his brains.'
Now I come
like a song on the night air,
spreading a tablecloth before every hunger,
pouring wine down the throat of thirst.
And you say,
'He staggers through the streets at noon
and fat glistens on his beard.'
You will not fast with John
or feast with me.
You will not repent in John's desert
or join hands around my table.
Just what will you do?"

John Shea

Before they could answer with their feet
and pivot on the heels of anger,
their backs bobbing away from his banquet,
Jesus threw a story around them
like a rope.

"Once there was a great man
who gave a great supper.
All was ready,
as poised as the breath of God
before the first day of life.
The servant was on the road,
dancing with the news of festivity,
banging the drums of party.
The first invited calculated:
    'I have bought a yard of land
    and I must measure it with my thumb.'
The second invited clucked:
    'I have bought five yoke of oxen
    and I must flick the flies from their ears.'
The third invited sighed:
    'I have married a young wife
    and I must hold her through the night.'
The servant returned, his hands
as empty as a man who has dropped a child.
He spoke each excuse in a whisper.
    'Out again!' the great man bellowed.
    'to hedge and highway, street and lane.
    Be as thorough as Noah.
    Persuade them all.'
The host waited at the door
and welcomed first a blind man.

The Indiscriminate Host

    'Sir, my eyes could not find your home
    but my nose found your food.'
Next a cripple greeted the great man.
    'The hill of your house is high, sir,
    but my one good leg is strong.'
Then a poor woman with a child of unflinching eyes
blocked the door like a star.
    'If with this food we talk and plot,
    I and my son will eat with you."
Then came a jumbling tumble of people
like they fell from an upended sack.
The servant was the last to dance in.
    'Am I a guest too?'
The great man stroked his chin.
    'Do you want to be?'
    'Yes!'
    'Then you are. But tell me:
    What did you say
    to all these people?
The servant stroked his chin.
    'I sang in the streets:
    There is a feast for all
    who want to feast with all.'
The great man turned to his eager guests.
    'In this house
    there is always a feast
    for those who seize it.' "

To Jesus
every person was a guest.
An invitation had gone out
from the heart of all life

to every heart within life
for does the rain discriminate
or the sun play favorites?
His voice was the music of welcome
in the ears of rejection;
his presence a silver setting in the slums
with linen napkins on the laps of lepers
and delicate china cups
cradled in calluses,
their thin rims pressed between lips,
thick and blistered with thirst.

At sunset
Jesus would haunt the marketplace,
saluting the unlikely.
    "You there,
    hurrying in the shadows!
    You there,
    dressed and without customers!
    You there,
    fearful that scorpions pop from chicken eggs
    and fish slither into snakes!
    You there,
    with the eyes of Cain!
    Eat with me tonight."
And somewhere amid the talk
of weather and crops and taxes
came a mercy
as sustaining as bread,
as intoxicating as wine.
They felt like the beauty of flowers
that do not toil

The Indiscriminate Host

and the grace of birds who ride the wind
without the strain of their wings.

Now those who know
the head from the foot of every table
were offended by this meal.
They regarded God as a knife
which divides the rotten from the righteous.
So they burst into the middle of forgiveness.
        "Ah! More guests!" cried Jesus.
    "Have respect," they threatened.
    "Do you know who you eat with?
    In the nature of things
    can what is out be in,
    can what is last be first?"
Jesus turned on them
like the knife of God they believed in.
        "In the nature of things
        if all are in, can anyone be out,
        if all are first, can anyone be last?"
And the pure gathered their robes around them
and went away into a draped room
where they agreed
that it was unpardonable of him
to make God
as accessible as a village well.

Even when Jesus was a guest
he slipped into being a host.
Once on his way through Jericho
a dwarf of a tax collector, Zacchaeus by name,
whose eyes were as tarnished as Roman coins

and whose hands were no bigger than a stolen purse
climbed a tree to spot Jesus.
But Jesus spied him.
     "Zacchaeus, hurry down.
     Tonight I dine at your house."
Now who is host and who is guest
when one invites and one accepts?
What can happen at a meal?
Can more than bread be shared?
Can more than wine be drunk?
In the morning Zacchaeus pulled the rusted key
from the center of his soul
and opened the locked boxes
where he kept the sweat of his country.
The people came and reclaimed
from the tall Zacchaeus
what the small man had taken.

Another time
a Pharisee, Simon by name,
whose fingernails were the white of ivory
and whose mind was a scroll of law
invited Jesus to a meal.
While they were at table
the storm of Magdelene,
all tears and hair and perfume,
broke upon the feet of Jesus.
Simon unrolled the parchment in his head.
   "If he was a prophet,
   he would know
   who this woman was
   who touched him."

The Indiscriminate Host

Jesus did know
but not what Simon knew.
    "I have something to say to you, Simon."
    "Speak, Teacher."
    "Two men owed money to a lender.
    One 500 coins, the other 50.
    The lender wrote off both debts.
    Of the debtors
    who was the most grateful?"

With Jesus
it always ended that way.
A hook in the heart
in the guise of a question.
    "Who proved neighbor to the man in need?"
    "What son did the will of the father?"
    "What will the King do to those men?"
    "Is it right to do good on the Sabbath?"
Now who is host and who is guest
when the one invited in turn invites?

It was the much in Magdelene that Jesus loved.
For, as Mark says,
    "He was too much for them."
Like a woman who loves too much,
like an ointment that costs too much
and is spilled too much,
like a seventy times seven God
who forgives too much,
like a seed that grows too much
and yields thirty
    sixty
    a hundred fold.

John Shea

It was the much in meals that Jesus loved.
The baskets of bread left over,
the fishes still to be eaten
and the table companions brimming,
amazed that they are cherished too much,
reeling at the extravagance of Jesus,
overtaken by the lavish God.

When the shadows were long
and the days of sharing short,
Jesus sent out his disciples
without cloak or coin,
possessing only his words
like troubadors with a single song.
They broke over Galilee
like a summer storm,
cleansing air and earth
and leaving a fragrance as fresh
as the time before the first scream.
They returned with the step of soldiers.
    "We have broken the back of pain,
    pushed ignorance into the sea,
    and stamped sour grapes into sweet wine."
Jesus said,
        "Come away with me and rest awhile,
        earthshakers,
        mountain movers,
        demon killers,
        sin stalkers."
But Mark says
the people pushed in on them so much
they could not even eat.

The Indiscriminate Host

So Jesus pulled them away
to a deserted place where they reclined
on the green grass of his soul.
    "We have done great things," they said.
     "Your feet are dusty.
    I will wash them" the master said.
    "We will make a time
of no hunger and no thirst."
     "People who would do away with hunger
     must themselves be hungry.
     Here is bread.
     People who would do away with thirst
     must themselves be thirsty.
     Here is wine.
     Hunger and thirst
     are the invitations
     God places in us
     to his banquet.
     Not 'no hunger' but hunger fed.
     Not 'no thirst' but thirst slaked.
     Not a time without needs
     but this time with needs met.
     Eat and remember!
     Or the earth you shake will swallow you,
     and the mountain you move will crush you,
     and the soul of the demon you kill
     will become your own,
     and the sin you stalk will in turn stalk you."
Jesus opened his hands
and a story fell live to the ground.
     "Once there was a rich man
     and the overgenerous earth rose to him

with the gift of a 1000 suppers of wheat.
At the sight of such abundance
his mind became a ledger
and he broke down his bins
and built a second set of barns
to house his new self-sufficiency.
'I will never be hungry again,' he shouted.
He never was. That night he died.
Eat and remember!"

"What would we forget?" they asked,
having already forgotten.

"That the short cannot grow by grunting
or the tall shrink with a wish.
That birds do not hold deeds
yet they own the sky.
That flowers have no mirrors
yet the sun kisses them.
That you are more than the birds
and more than the flowers
and that God barbers even the bald.
Worry the Kingdom to birth
and not yourself to death.
Eat and remember!"

Much later
Peter did remember that
after Jesus had reached a long arm
into the hole of death
and pulled Jairus' daughter back by the hair
he said,

"She is alive and hungry.
Feed her."

On the night
when the one who broke bread with Jesus
also broke bond with him,
Jesus gathered his friends
for the last wine before the grape of the Kingdom.
    "Who is the master?" the master asked.
  "You are."
    "Who are the servants?"
"We are," the servants replied.
Then Jesus reversed his robe into an apron
and poured water on their feet
which ran into the rivers of their legs
and rushed for the home of the heart.
They were embarrassed
that he was so poured out,
squandering himself on them,
one with the water of their freshness,
as spent as the time
he had wept Lazarus to life.
So Peter said,
  "Not me!"
    "Can so reluctant a guest
    ever be hosted?" asked Jesus.
    "Do not hold back.
    Allow the mind a morning in a meadow of sun.
    Allow the soul an afternoon of memory.
    The grain the improvident God throws to the wind
    the air harvests.
    The seed the wild God buries in the ground

becomes a tree of shade.
Drink! Do not tongue taste the wine of God.
Eat! Do not teeth tease the bread of God.
Give yourself to my love."
"Then not only my feet
but hands and head as well."
"Ah, too much!" Jesus laughed.
"God is here."
At the meal
Jesus said,
    "My friends,
    hold onto life with an open hand
    as I hold this bread and wine.
    This bread is our food.
    This wine is our drink.
    This meal is our fellowship.
    So we hand over to the Giver of Life
    the music our muscles make,
    the kisses that bring peace,
    the sounds that swell the heart.
    But this bread is my body broken.
    This wine is my blood outpoured.
    This meal is our sacrifice.
    So we hand over to the Giver of Life
    the eyes that squint back,
    the hands that do not reach out,
    the barricaded mind, the hoarding heart.
    All we are we offer.
    Life received as a gift
    is given up as a gift."

Then there was a garden without fragrance
and a man with cold lips
and a high priest with a ripped robe

The Indiscriminate Host

and a governor with glistening hands
and a disciple with a labyrinthine lie
and a carpenter put back to work.

After Jesus had passed through the dark door,
his friends returned
to what they knew best,
Galilee and the sea.
One evening Peter said,
  "I am going out to weep."
But they thought he said,
  "I am going out to fish."
So they went with him
and they wept and fished the night away,
catching nothing but their tears.
With the dawn
came a fire on the shore
and the smell of fish across the water.
Through the mist
a man was crumbled over coals.
He rose
like an arrow from the bow of the earth,
like an open hand in a time of war,
like the smoke of an undying sacrifice
and turned.
    "Come and eat your meal."
No one, John says, presumed to inquire,
  "Who are you?"
They knew who it was.
The host had returned.

That is why we meet together
with food and drink between us.
As God would not let go of Jesus

in the hour of his death,
his friends would not let go of him
in the hour of his glory.
Down to this day
we break the bread of his absence
and hope
and drink the wine of his presence
and live.

Chapter Six

The Son Who Must Die

The Galilean stood high on the hill,
alone on the hill,
safe on the hill,
and he did not like it.
   Like a God, Paul sang,
   who was high in the heavens,
   alone in the heavens,
   safe in the heavens,
   and one day looked down
   to catch every human eye looking up
   and the slow tear of the sky God began.
   From toes to knees
   the tear was compassion
   for the blood
   which would never again find veins.
   From knees to chest
   the tear was desire
   to dance in the circle of beauty.
   From chest to eyes
   the tear was love
   to kiss us in the cave of death.
   From eye to earth
   the tear became
Jesus
watching the brown river below him
breaking against the waist of the Baptist

who was burying sinners with his shovel hands
then ripping them repentant from their Jordan graves
with a force more violent than birth.
The afternoon sun was at Jesus' back
so his shadow preceded him down the hill
like a spirit guiding him toward John.
Jesus pushed into the eddies of people,
at home in the swirls of conversion.

When John saw him,
a dark, bent memory
of a greeting long ago
lept inside him.
He moved like a man
with only a second of life left
and pushed down on the burning shoulders
of the grown child of Mary's song.
The waters covered Jesus like a cloud.
From the dark sky beneath the Jordan
God rained down the secret name
and Jesus broke the surface,
not gasping for air
but bursting breath,
exhaling the oxygen God gives
to those he drowns.
　　"I heard the name," John said.
　　"It was lamb."
For a moment
the fist of the Baptist's heart relaxed,
his fingers loosened one by one
like a man at the end of the day
who lays away the sledge

The Son Who Must Die

that pounded a mountain into pavement,
a highway for the feet of good news.
The newly named one was already gone,
pushing forcefully toward shore,
his hands paddling the water behind him,
a man with a mission in his mind.

The waters were as crowded
as a public square of execution;
yet none but John
and the thin man on the shore
who sat coiled
beneath a withered fig tree
heard a name.
The thin man rose, straightening to a stick,
and stretched a hand to the hurrying man,
scrambling up the bank.
   "I heard a name. What did John
   say it was?
His voice was without music,
just a heavy noise
like the thud of a falling man.
      "John said lamb."
   "Lamb? Is John so eager for slaughter?
I heard Messiah."
      "The name was Son," Jesus said.
   "Yes, of course. Son.
Walk with me awhile. Shake the Jordan
from your ears. Dry your clothes.
   Breathe without the river in your nose."
The thin man had been chewing a fig.
He spit the juiceless skin into the river

and turned quickly on Jesus
like a man who had rolled up his sleeves
and was about to wrestle.
  "You lean like a wood carrier.
Are you a carpenter?"
    "Yes."
"There were many in the water.
Are you sure the name
was meant for you?"
    "It is mine."
"Strange! God seldom chooses carpenters
to do his hammering."
    "Is God a hammer then?"
"He's not a nail. He makes things be
what they are not. You know, barren women
bearing sons. Why a son of his
could force rock to become bread.
No sturdy stone
that has beat off wind and sun
wants the humiliating fate of grain,
disappearing into digestion.
Try it. These rocks are available
for dinner. Then we will know
if you are the Son of Muscle."
    "Are you then concerned about bread?"
Jesus hoped he was a friend.
  "I am not a baker, Jesus. My interest is
in ropes and tight spaces,
in how things get hemmed in
and in how hands squeeze.
How does power push, Jesus?"
    "I think it pulls."
"Either way, it gets its way."

The Son Who Must Die

"Is the mission of the Son then
to bend arms?"
"If the nature of the Father
is to bend knees."
They were now far into the desert.
The day was gone
and the night was the howls of wild beasts
punctuating the sentences of the thin man.
   "With a new name
   must come a new game."
      "The game of the name?"
"What else? The temple is the house of God.
Is not the Son welcome in the Father's home.
Go to the pinnacle and float down
before the priests and people."
      "Does the Son presume to fly?
"Does the Father not own the air? 'Angels
will support you.' David's words, none better.
      "It is not the word of the water."
"Think of it. The eyes of the people glazed.
Their mouths opening and closing on your name.
They will follow you to conquest."
      "Is the Father then a blank stare
      and the Son a hypnotist?
      Is the Father a Lord of War
      and the Son a General of Blood?"
"All right! How do you
propose to fight?
      "Like the Father loves."
The thin man stepped back,
his hands disappeared into the sleeves of his robe
and he faded into forty freezing nights
and forty feverish days

which brought Jesus exhausted
back to the Jordan
whose swift flow of sins to the sea
had ceased.
Herod had John.

The cry "Repent!" slid quickly through the bars,
climbed the stone stairs of the dungeon,
overrode the injustice of the judgment hall
and echoed in the silkened rooms of Herodias.
The sword was soon for John.
So he sent his disciples
to the man of the name
to check what his ears had heard.
   "Are you the one who is to come
   or shall we look for another?"
A thin voice inside Jesus
as flat and hard as a palm
that slaps an innocent man
urged,
   "Tell them
   you are a white horse of victory
   which they will ride to glory."
Instead Jesus said,
    "What do you see?"
And their eyes ran away with their faces
at the mute filibustering,
the lame high-jumping,
the blind painting rainbows,
the deaf with perfect pitch,
and the poor picnicking
in the fields of plenty.
The Son of God was walking the world.

The Son Who Must Die

One Sabbath day
a man with a withered arm
as stunted and gnarled
as a washed up branch on a beach
longed to touch Jesus.
Jesus grabbed his dangling fingers
and pulled his arm
till it filled his sleeve.
The authorities screamed,
  "Do you think
  you have the right
  to make muscles
  on the day
  God made nothing?"
Jesus raised his own arm
and the grumbling ground down.
    "God lives in the moments of new muscle,
    at the junctures of justice,
    when time is twisting
    and the kaleidoscope turning.
    God is dough bursting into bread,
    seeds stretching into trees,
    spring promenading into summer.
    The Kingdom that comes transforms what is,
    the lethargic dance with its energy.
    If the Father is washing the world new,
    does not the Son kiss it dry?
    If the Father is breaking chains like thread,
    does not the Son shout, "Freedom!"
    If the Father claps his hands
    for the feast to begin,
    is not the Son host, servant and music?"

John Shea

"The law is clear,"
said those who knew the law.
"You have sinned."
    "The times are clear,"
    said the one who knew the times.
    "God is near.
    You read the weather in the sky
    but not the malice in your hearts.
    To the blast of trumpets
    you pass out pennies.
    You weigh herbs on golden scales
    lest God be cheated on his tithe
    but you ladle the soup of the poor
    with shallow spoons.
    The outside of the cup you shine
    till your face shines back.
    But inside a gnat and camel
    swim and sip and sing old favorites.
    Horrified, you strain the fastidious gnat
    and proceed to drink the mountainous camel.
    First your mouth slurps in the surprised head.
    The long, hairy neck slides easily down,
    followed by the twin humps
    which salute the adams' apple as they pass.
    Finally, the four legs,
    heels following head,
    disappear."
The crowd roared
at righteousness
so rightly rendered.
    "Then with a thunderous belch you bolt forward
    in a two-stage, undulating rhythm,

punctuating your gossip with a bray,
galloping toward the eye of a needle
which is your only passage to salvation."

The people now laughed openly
at the whitewashed ways of those who held power.
So the authorities met secretly
and said,
   "Not for us, but for the people!
   Not for us, but for the law!
   Not for us, but for the faith!
   Not for us, but for the children!
   This man must die!"

Another time
Jesus smeared God like mud
on the eyes of a man born blind
and pushed him toward the pool of Siloam.
The blind man splashed his eyes
and stared into the rippling reflection
of the face he had only felt.
First he did a handstand, then a cartwheel,
and rounded off his joy
with a series of summersaults.
He ran to his neighbors,
singing the news.
They said,
   "You look like the blind beggar
   but we cannot be sure."
The problem was never
that he was blind
and could not look out

but that they could see
and did not look in.
  "I am the one, the seeing blind!"
They seized him in mid cartwheel
and dragged him to the authorities.
  "What do you think
  of the man who made the mud?"
But the man born blind
was staring at a green vase.
His mouth was open slightly
as if he was being fed by its color.
  "He is a sinner," said a priest
  who knew what pleased God's eyes.
  "Can one who lights candles in the eyes of night
  not have the fire of God in his hands?"
  said the man fondling the green vase.
The priests murmurred
and sent for his parents
who looked their son
straight in his new eyes
and said,
  "Looks like our son.
  But he is old enough
  to speak for himself."
Off the hook they hurried home.
  "All I know," said the man
  with the green vase tucked under his robe,
  "is that I was blind
  and now I see."
But with his new eyes
came a turbulence in his soul
as if the man who calmed one sea
turned another to storm.

The Son Who Must Die

So before those who locked knowledge in a small room
and kept the key on a string around their neck
he launched into a theology of sin and salvation.
It was then
that the full horror of the miracle
visited the priests.
   "You, steeped in sin, lecture us!"
They tore him from the podium
and threw him into the street
where a man was rubbing mud from his hands.
     "How did it go?"
   "I talked back."
The man with new eyes
took in every laughing line
on the face of the Son
who was as happy as a free man
dancing on the far side of the Red Sea.

It was on the way to the dead girl's house
that new dice tumbled from the cup
and all the gamblers
save one
scrambled.
The people jostled against Jesus,
mobbing their way toward miracle.
They moved as one through the streets
as if he carried all of them with each step.
Suddenly Jesus howled.
A whip had unravelled
from as far away as the future of God
and found his naked back.
    "Who touched me?"
   "Who did not?" said Peter.

"The crowd is all over us."
    "Someone touched me.
    Power went out from me."
And he waited in the middle of the street
like a man who had fallen
and was on his feet again.
Finally a woman said,
    "I touched you."
        "Are you cured?"
    "Yes."
        "Go in peace."
She went in peace
but Jesus did not.

Instead
he sought out the mountains
and walked them through the night.
He retreated to deserted places
where he was as sealed off
as a man under water.
He prayed like a prosecutor,
placing God in the dock
and parading the evidence of agony before him.
God made no defense but cried fiercely.
Jesus asked,
        "Is the power to heal
        the power to suffer?
        Why when power went out,
        did pain come in?"
Then God spoke all the words that were ever spoken
but the only word Jesus heard was Son.

In the district of the ten Cities
they brought a deaf mute to Jesus.

The Son Who Must Die

He sighed at the sight of the man
and seized him like a wrestler.
He groaned aloud
and the crowd heard.
    "Open his ears!
    Untie his tongue!"
But the echo in the soul of Jesus was:
    "Close my ears!
    Knot my tongue!"
As the noise of creation honked and rumbled
down the tunnels of the man's ears,
the inner world of Jesus slammed shut
as if a great stone had been rolled across it.
As the mute man broke into songs of praise,
the mouth of a 1000 stories
had not one one word in it.
Then they brought a blind man to Jesus
and he pressed his thumbs into the sightless sockets.
As the man swam in color,
Jesus went as dark as a starless sky.
The lepers came
and left their scales on his back.
The cripples crutched in
and abandoned their twisted muscles in his legs.
In the middle of sleep
sinners shook him awake with their shame
and then left for home and rest.
The Son of God was walking the world.

After a night of prayer with the God
who bargains for more than he gets,
Jesus asked his disciples:
    "Who do people
    say that I am?"

"The Baptist from the grave," said Andrew.
"Elijah from the sky," said Philip.
"The Prophet of No More Days," said John.
     "And you,
     who do you
     say that I am?"
As usual,
Peter covered the silence.
     "The Son of the Living God."
     "Yes!
     And the Son of the Living God
     is faithful unto death.
     We go to Jerusalem."
The disciples searched the ground for words.
Peter took Jesus aside and reasoned with him
in a voice that never knew a song.
     "Master,
     Jerusalem is a basket of snakes.
     For the moment
     let us go to Galilee
     and fish and pray and dream a tearless city.
     In a year
     when God's time has been balm for sore hearts,
     the priests will be pacified
     and we will return renewed
     to preach the Kingdom."
     "It is the Kingdom that preaches us, Peter."
"Then to Jerusalem and glory!
You are the Holy One of God.
God will guard you."
Peter's voice was now as sharp
as a stick jabbed in the ribs of a criminal.

The Son Who Must Die

"Peter,
the Father is not the armor the Son wears.
The Son is the vulnerability of God,
as defenseless as a child,
as unprotected as a man with outstretched arms.
Then Jesus gathered his friends around him,
not under the wings of a hen
who shelters and broods
but under the wings of the eagle God
who solos on the high winds of heaven.
"My friends,
if the Father takes all things into himself
so that all might go out from him,
what must the Son do?"
Peter did not know.
Magdelene did not know.
All the disciples,
save Judas,
did not know.

Astride a borrowed donkey
whose hooves trampled the royal palms
and cheered by the poor who have no voice
and rocks that have recently learned to shout,
Jesus arrived at the feast of a liberation long gone
with the hope of a liberation yet to come.
The Son
whose hands never left the plow
and who pushed past fields of the dead
burying their own
moved with the anger of a long lost heir
into the traffic of the temple.

John Shea

The priest of the whip and the dream
shouted over the clatter of coins
at the fleeing priests of smoke and magic.
    "Not for the people, but for you!
    Not for the law, but for you!
    Not for the faith, but for you!
    Not for the children, but for you!
    I must die!"

So Annas whispered in the ear of Caiaphas
and Caiaphas whispered in the ear of Herod
and Herod whispered in the ear of Pilate
and the thin man hunted the midnight streets
till he found him awake in the garden of sleep
and whispered in the ear of Jesus
who screamed at the night.
    "Send twelve legions of angels
    and I will crush them."
But the voice was not his own.
It had no ring to it,
like someone had ripped
the tongue from a great bell.
Jesus prayed again,
    "Your will is my blood.
    You wish is my breath."
And the music of the water returned
and with it the name the Jordan gave him.

Then a tree without leaves
and nails against the carpenter
and cracked lips of gall
and the thin man turned legion,

The Son Who Must Die

his voice splintered into a 1000 thorns,
each one piercing the darkness of noon.
　　"If you are the Son of God,
　　climb down from that cross;
　　and dance in the temple air
　　or bake rocks into bread
　　or step on the neck of the world
　　or escape into the desert
　　and starve yourself into heaven."
But Jesus held fast
to the life he was losing.
It was the centurion of many crucifixions
who saw in the man on the edge of the world
the Son of the God of everlasting embrace.
　　"Truly, this was the Son of Love."
Then he ran a lance into the side
of the man who would not come down.
The blood of Jesus and the water of the Jordan
flowed as one stream down the cross,
soaking through the earth
with the determination of a journey,
carrying the Son
to the unmoving center of the universe.

Chapter Seven

The Storyteller of God

The curtain of the sanctuary
was not torn in two
at the death of Jesus.
It happened years earlier.
Jesus had slipped past the temple guards
and cut the veil of the Holy of Holies
like the back of a desert tent
to free the bound and gagged God.
Once inside
he shouted the secret-sacred name of God,
the name no mouth could speak without burning,
the name that matched the face
whose sight was death.
But there was no answer,
not even the small voice
which Elijah heard outside the cave.
Then Jesus whispered,
     "Abba!"
and the conspirator God
filled both his hands with seed
which Jesus spread over Palestine
like a lunatic farmer,
giving the road and rock
an equal chance with the fertile field
to go white with harvest.
God was taking root.

The Storyteller of God

The seed of God grew in secret
and went the way of wheat
into the blood and sinew of unsuspecting people.
So when they came to Jesus
to see when God would come,
he unwrapped the gift already there.
    "See the clouds! They gather for storm,
    menacing the west, thundering for attention.
    Till with a switch of wind we turn,
    then scatter for shelter.
    If they tell you
    the Kingdom comes like that . . ."
Jesus rubbed his hands in delight.
He loved suspense.
    "Do not believe it!"
The people groaned.
    "Get to the point."
    "Remember the days of dust in the distance.
    Low in the skies were the clouds of marching feet;
    soldiers with bleeding eyes were near.
    We would bury our coins in the earth
    and bar the door.
    If they tell you
    the Kingdom comes like that . . ."
Jesus paused.
    "On with it!" the crowd shouted.
    "Do not believe it!"
    "Jesus, speak plainly!"
The people were impatient for God.
They wanted him to arrive with the force of a spear.
    "Let the one with eyes see!"
Jesus swept his arm
over the heads of all.

John Shea

"Let the one with ears hear!
God is among us.
He is outin-withside,
inhind-befront,
overneath-underhead.
Do not try to tie him
to a stake and stare.
Catch the beauty
of the butterfly God
on the wing.
He is what we have but cannot hold,
what we dwell within but cannot domesticate,
a home with unexplored rooms,
a foreign land with warmth."
The crowd looked at one another,
shook their heads,
and returned to working and making love.
Now the absence of God
is as obvious as a boxer's nose
which brings us to the putty of God's nose.
The nose of God,
as any churchman will tell you,
is Roman, an angular line
which arrives at a mouth
poised for pulpit performance.
But in the wind that blows where it will
his nose turns proudly pug
and perched on the plateau
is an angel who holds an umbrella
lest a sudden deluge drown God
and dose the grey-red fire of the stogy
which puffs from his mouth
the smoke signals of an old time pol.

The Storyteller of God

The fickleness of God's nose
would make a sculptor cry.
Which, of course, was Jesus' point.

And so
by every fire and shore,
in marketplace and on hillside,
with the children of the street
and the masters of the law
Jesus told stories of God
which were really stories of people
who for the moment
had borrowed the nose of God
to sniff the cinnamon earth
or who were working with the hands of God
   like a poor farmer
      scratching the gravelly ground for a mouthful
      when suddenly
      he hears a clunk,
      a box where it shouldn't be,
      and inside a rocking chair
      for the porch of retirement;
or who were walking with the feet of God
   like a pearl merchant forever on the road
   who turns a leg-weary corner and
   suddenly
   finds the milk white eye of perfection
   winking at him with the promise of home;
or who were searching with the eyes of God
   like a housewife atwit,
   her money somewhere but where,
   scouring the house with a candle when
   suddenly

the coin leaps from its hiding place
into her eye.
or who were laughing with the mouth of God
like shepherds,
their beards dripping beer,
retelling the story of the lost lamb
suddenly
found and slung
over the returning shoulders of joy.

People came, to Jesus
with God in their pockets
and their pockets sewn tight.
"Master,
if only people would pray
as the law prescribes."
And suddenly
they were in the company of two men
arriving at the temple to pray.
One stood in front,
eye to eye with God,
the shawl of righteousness around him.
His prayer was a textbook of liturgy.
"Thank God,
I am not like those," he prayed,
following step one
and separating himself from the impure,
"who creep into the wrong bed
and dip into the wrong purse
and speak with the wrong words.
Thank God,
I am a smile of many teeth," he prayed,
following step two

and giving an account,
"and tithe every penny
and pray the sun up in the morning
and down at night
and fast for the pleasure of you,
my God."
The man in the back
crouched low
lest the roof of God fall on him.
"Mercy," he prayed,
not knowing the form.
"Mercy," he prayed,
too sorry to worry.
"Mercy," he prayed,
tears his only tithe.
"Which man has the ear of God?"
asked the man who was the word of God.
"The one in front who prayed
the way he should."
They all nodded in agreement.
"The one in the back who prayed
the only way he could."
The crowd stared hard at Jesus.
He was not
who at first
he seemed.
He was a man
they would like to push
to the edge of a cliff.

In the wake of Jesus' stories
the mind was a library
torn by storm;

John Shea

the heart was a deer
with the thirst of summer.
The stories were snow from a cloudless sky,
wine from vats of water,
a feast from the pickings of the poor;
as unexpected
as an embrace for a renegade
or a bandage from a foe.

Who would think that
a son who says,
   "Yes! I will work in the field."
would hide in a tavern;
and a son who says,
   "No! I will not go."
would plough the land.
Who would think that
an afternoon stroller
would find in his palm the pay
given to workers
who bear the heat of the day.
Who would think that
Dives would want for a finger of water
and Lazarus would dine with Abraham.
Who would think that
a struck cheek would ask for more
and a man stripped of his tunic
would strip himself of his cloak.

And who would think that
a father would be foolish enough
to let his wealth roll down his arms
into the twenty fingers of his two sons.

The Storyteller of God

And who would think that
when he saw the younger one
who took the money and ran
trudging toward home,
rehearsing the script of a slave,
   "Father, no son here,
   only sin.
   Hire me."
he would race down the hill
the boy would not have to crawl up
and run upon the runaway
with the robe and ring and sandals of sonship,
calling for the feast to begin.
And who would think that
the father would climb the hill of forgiveness
he had just run down
to meet the older one
who took the money and stayed
and who was as bitter as a slave,
   "What have you done for me
   who works like a hired hand?"
And who would think that
for a second time the father would reach out
for a son with no party in his soul
to hold him in joy
and whisper to him welcome.

No one would think these things
except the storyteller of God.

Go then
to the man who saw the wind
and ask,

John Shea

"Master,
who is my neighbor?"
And suddenly
you are on the road
that winds from Jerusalem to Jericho.
Clubs rush from the bushes
and the bright day of journey turns sunless.
You wake in the ditch,
as broken as firewood,
as helpless as a ram on the altar.
A face enters your blurred eyes.
It is the priest of the temple,
the tassles of his robe
pulled above the dust of the road.
He is passing you by,
hurrying to ceremony.
Another face
belonging to a teacher of wisdom
is studying you from the road.
You reach out an arm of pain
but he sees no wisdom in taking it.
Another approaches.
It is the face of the one you hate,
probably one of those who beat you,
come back to finish it.
Strange!
You see your tears in his eyes.
His large hands are under you.
You are out of the ditch!
The arms of your enemy
are carrying you to health.

Go then to the man
with no rock in his hand

The Storyteller of God

and ask,
  "Master,
  what is God like?"
And suddenly
it is late at night
and a distant knocking
is pulling you from the world of dream.
The voice of your friend is pleading.
  "Lend me three loaves.
  "I have late night guests."
  "Go away," you say.
  "I am in bed."
But the wood continues to bang
with the persistence of a covenant oath.
So you throw back the covers of warmth.
  "All right!" you mutter,
  like a man saying,
  "Not my will but yours!"
You hand the bread of hospitality
to the smiling but shivering man outside,
whose scraped knuckles belong to God.

Or suddenly
you are gowned in power,
a judge whose verdicts are
as slick as well worn coins.
All salute you in the marketplace
and from their sleeves
pull presents to please you.
Except a certain widow with a certain case
who in the morning waits before your door
and in the court nags
your heartless logic with her need
and at night weeps outside your garden.

John Shea

One day,
wearied by her words,
you say,
   "All right!"
You give justice to the widow
whose ceaseless tongue belongs to God.

Go then to the man
who scribbles in the sand
and ask,
   "Master,
   what are the times
   we live in?"
And suddenly
you are a servant
who keeps his master's books
and makes the figures dance
to the music of your arithmetic.
The grapevine squeezes out the word:
   "The master means to fire you."
Your soft hands cannot dig ditches
and your stiff neck will not beg.
What will you do,
O man in crisis?

For a second time
you are a servant
with the master's money in your keep.
Before his journey
the hard hands of the master
which sow what they do not reap
and gather what they have not scattered

stuff silver in your pocket
for more than good keeping.
It would be safe
to bury the coins in the earth
with the lie
that they will turn to seed.
What will you do,
O man in crisis?

Jesus told so many stories
that he became one,
the story of the growing God
beneath the heart of the virgin.

The young girl of the overshadowing kiss
worries the supernatural hills of Judah
to visit the barren womb of Elizabeth
where the God who made Sarah laugh
is whispering jokes to embryonic John.
Even then
John jumped at Jesus.
And Elizabeth cried,
    "Blessed!"
And the incredulous tongue of Zachary
tied by the stern belief of an angel
is undone by the birth of his son
and, as straight as a path before the Lord,
cries,
    "Blessed!"
And Mary,
filled with the fragrance of God,
her hair undone in the wind

that blows where it will,
sings of a love that never forgets
and a justice that never relents.

Then
at a homeless time of forced travel
in a stable on the edge of the world
a child who has nowhere to lay his head
is swaddled in the rags of the poor
and warmed with the straw of beasts.
Shepherds coaxed by a night of voices
and wise men dragged by a dancing star
watch new born arms beat the air,
conducting angels only children see.
Beneath the skies that sing
the virgin mother holds the child of the song.

Then
the everlasting enmity
between kings and babies,
the sword chasing and slaughtering
what cannot be killed,
the angel pouring haste
into the sleeping ear of Joseph.
  "Run!
  Take Mary!
  Run!
  Take the child!
  Run!"
And running
Mary treasured Jesus,
feeding him slices of her heart
till the whisper of the handmaiden,

The Storyteller of God

"Your will be done."
became the shout of the Son,
  "Your Kingdom come."
And running,
she watched the infant eyes
that closed against the Egypt sun
give way to a young man's stare
into the burning sky of Nazareth.
And running,
she stayed at the edges
of his towering days,
the mother outside who constantly sees him.
And running,
she arrived
at the afternoon of Simeon's sword,
the mother at the cross who sorrowing holds him.

First,
there was a Friday night of black rain
as if God had forgotten his promise to Noah.

Next,
there was a century of a Saturday,
a day that never saw him smile.
Finally,
near the end of the longest night
before a stone the size of twelve men
around a fire that gave off cold
three hooded forms stood watch.

There is no fat
on the face and hands
of the first to speak.

John Shea

His mouth is a black hole
and each word echoes
like it travelled a great hollow tunnel
to arrive at his lips.
　"Goals rule means.
　Ends mock middles.
　Graves rock cradles.
　Irrefutable.
　I, Death, stand at the end
　but my shadow darkens the start.
　In the bridal bed I whisper
　how the old use covers for warmth
　and in the muscle days of youth
　I remind them how the aged fumble
　with the cap on the aspirin bottle.
　I am wearied by this argument.
　It is my power that is unparalleled.
　It is a question of the largest mouth.
　The rabbit eats the grass.
　The fox eats the rabbit.
　Man eats the fox.
　And I eat man.
　He who eats last
　dines forever.
　So
　if a passer-by would ask
　who rules this life,
　point him to this stone
　and tell him I am inside
　disassembling the handiwork of God."

　"Eloquently pleaded, Death."
The lounging figure by the fire

raises a palm of protestation.
"But falsely asserted.
It is true
you are as inescapable as skin.
But that makes you a mere fact,
painful perhaps but insignificant.
Now with myself it is different.
I, Sin, parade as possibility.
I manure the dreams of the young
and wait for a harvest of betrayal.
When their first kiss turns to bite
or they torch a reputation
or mix a motive
or watch a belly bloat
to the size of an empty bowl
or add a column so the bottom figures
tumble effortlessly into their pockets,
then I say,
'Buy silk suits and ties of gold
so no one will know
the electricity of your mind is greed
and the seventy beats of your pulse are lust
and the movement of your muscles mere envy.'
I reign from the inside,
severing the nerve,
marshmallowing the mind,
bronzing the heart.
So
if a passer-by would ask
who rules this life,
point him to this stone
and tell him I am inside
claiming the failed dreamer.

John Shea

No sooner had Sin stopped
than Fate was on his feet.
  "Fact or possibility, please!
  The rain shines and the sun falls,
  tomorrow is today and today yesterday.
  I write
  and the scribbled lines of men
  are written.
  I do not rattle bones
  like you, Death.
  Or wait for clouds to gather
  in the blue eyes of innocence
  like you, Sin.
  I tell them
  bones and flesh are the same
  and blue always turns to grey.
  I have twin straws dipped deep
  into their hope and freedom
  and I drain them empty of struggle,
  their faces whitening into resignation.
  My message swims in their ears
  like a rock concert:
  'Kiss the earth!
  Throw no dust into the wind!
  Marrionettes are not masters!'
  So
  if a passer-by would ask
  who rules this life,
  point him to this stone
  and tell him I am inside
  overseeing what was meant to be.

Now the sun,
which Ecclesiastes says always rises,

broke the night of fierce debate
but no rooster greeted it.
Instead
a stone the size of twelve men
moved like a mountain on its way to the sea
and on the fresh wind of morning
came the Son of Man,
his shroud a wedding garment,
his feet between earth and air in dance.
Death, Sin, and Fate poured rhetoric
into the stirring air about them
but the silent Son of God only danced
to music beyond their words.
He whirled around Death
and with each turn
Death himself grew old
till with a last, unbelievable look
he saw no more.
Then wordless
Christ spun around the words of Sin
till a stammer started, sound choked,
and finally there was only a mouth
without a voice.
Next Fate heard the risen footsteps
and frost formed on his tongue.
As Christ lept before him,
he froze in mid-syllable,
iced by the warmth of God.

Now
there was only the morning
and the dancing man of the broken tomb.
The story says
he dances still.

That is why
down to this day
we lean over the beds of our babies
and in the seconds before sleep
tell the story of the undying dancing man
so the dream of Jesus will carry them to dawn.

Afterword

VERY few get through high school without hearing Plato's warning that the unexamined life is not worth living. Very few get through middle age without the secret sigh that the unexamined life is the only one worth living. To sail or muddle through depending on the circumstances seems, on the face of it, to be an eminently sensible way of going about life.

The trouble begins with the suspicion that we are here to do more than survive. Since, whether we go gentle or kicking into that good night, we *do* go into that good night, perhaps the time of our striving is meant to be more than a losing duel with death. Perhaps, the mind surmises, the mystery of our coming and going is a mission, a mandate, a destiny. Perhaps, the heart intuits, we are bonded to an Ultimate Truth which knows and calls us, loves and critiques us. This head and heart suspicion is the trembling hope and joyous trouble we call God.

Flannery O'Connor once remarked of a writer's prose that it was so sensitive that you constantly wondered if what he was describing was actually *there*. Belief in God is under the same sentence of sensitivity. To stay within the Christian tradition we must affirm simultaneously the immanence and transcendence of God. No matter how we may shout that the present situation is divorced from God (his fullness being either in the past or the future), we must also maintain a presence, however elusive. No matter how rapturous our songs about God's embrace, we must also pine for the God who is not yet among us. The presence of God to our lives means that we are under way; the absence of God means that we are unfinished. Faith can never move out of the space where absence and presence intersect.

Faith in God yields a double self-understanding. We experience ourselves as both gift and task. At some times we receive ourselves as funded from beyond; at other times we receive ourselves as enticed from beyond. E. B. White once reflected that people are torn by two powerful drives: the desire to enjoy the world and the urge to set it straight. These two drives cannot be successfully reconciled but greatness lies in the struggle to respond to both of them. To live out of God is to live in the alternating rhythms of enjoyment and transformation. It is to relish the gift of ourselves as it abundantly arrives and to engage in the task of ourselves as it imperatively calls. Faith makes us a people of both Sabbath delight and Kingdom passion.

The fullness of both gift and task is Jesus. He stands at the beginning of the Christian way of responding to the mystery of life. And whatever else the story of the Second Coming may mean, it is the adamant conviction that he will stand at the end. No matter what frontiers are crossed or what worlds come about, we will not outgrow Jesus. The one who initiated will be the one who finishes. Lest this alpha and omega tribute turn to mere flattery, we must make Jesus not only the beginning and the end but also the middle. This is the fundamental and irreplaceable meaning of faith in Jesus. We must resort to him. We must take our lives to his and think, feel, and act out of the interaction. In this way our faith is Christian for we approach and appropriate our relationship to God and all other realities through Jesus who is the Christ.

The writer of Proverbs modestly admits that four things baffle him.

> the way of an eagle in the sky,
>> the way of a serpent on a rock,
> the way of a ship in the heart of the sea
>> and the way of a man with maiden.

The puzzle that concerns us is a ship in the *heart* of the sea. In ancient times ships stayed close to the coast, using the sight of land to direct their journey. The heart of the sea was its unknown center, far from shore, terrifying to think of and impossible to navigate. The biblical image of heart often stands for the unknown and the hidden. Perhaps it is this that the Johannine Christ, whose words triggered this meditation on faith, commands us not to be troubled by.

> Do not let the unknown trouble you!
> Have faith in God
> and faith in me.

NOTES

Chapter One

[1] Friedrich Nietzche, *Joyful Wisdom*, p. 233. Quoted in Ray L. Hart, *Unfinished Man and the Imagination* (New York: Herder and Herder, 1968), p. 237.

[2] Alfred North Whitehead, *Process and Reality* (The Macmillan Co.: New York, 1929), p. 526.

[3] James Olney, *Metaphors of Self: The Meaning of Autobiography* (Princeton, New Jersey: Princeton University Press, 1972), p. vii.

[4] Karl Rahner, *Foundations of Christian Faith* (New York: The Seabury Press, 1978), p. 83.

[5] Edward Schillebeeckx, *God and Man* (New York: Sheed and Ward, 1969), p. 164.

[6] Ibid., 164.

[7] For a fuller treatment of how we become aware of our relationship to Mystery consult John Shea, *Stories of God* (Chicago: Thomas More Press, 1978), pp. 11-39.

[8] Thomas Fawcett, *The Symbolic Language of Religion* (Minneapolis, Minnesota: Augsburg Publishing House, 1971), p. 170.

[9] Edward Schillebeeckx, *Jesus* (New York: The Seabury Press, 1979), p. 627.

[10] Fawcett, 170.

[11] Ibid., 170.

[12] Flannery O'Connor, *Everything That Rises Must Converge* (New York: Farrar, Straus and Giroux, 1965), pp. 217-18.

[13] Langdon Gilkey, *How the Church Can Minister to the World Without Losing Itself* (New York: Harper & Row, 1964), p. 134.

[14] Paul Ricoeur, *The Symbolism of Evil* (Boston: Beacon Press, 1967), p. 354.

[15] Eugene T. Gendlin, *Experiencing and the Creation of Meaning* (Glencoe, Illinois: The Free Press, 1962), p. 5.

[16] William Temple. Quoted in *A Treasury of Quotations on Christian Themes* (New York: The Seabury Press, 1975), p. 29.

[17] Christophe Luthardt. Quoted in Victor Gollancz, *A Year of Grace* (London: Penguin Books, 1959), p. 430.

Chapter Two

[1] Kirsopp Lake. Quoted in *A Treasury of Quotations on Christian Themes* (New York: The Seabury Press, 1975), p. 168.

[2] Tennesse Williams, *Suddenly Last Summer.* Quoted in Gordon D. Kaufman, *Systematic Theology: A Historicist Perspective* (New York: Charles Scribner's Sons, 1968), p. 310.

[3] D. H. Lawrence, *Women in Love.* Quoted in Brian Wicker, *The Story-Shaped* World (Notre Dame, Indiana: University of Notre Dame Press, 1975), p. 122.

[4] George Santayana, *The Life of Reason* (New York: Charles Scribner's Sons, 1905).

[5] Hans Kung, *On Being a Christian* (New York: Doubleday & Company, 1976), p. 74.

[6] John Bowker, *The Sense of God* (Clarendon Press, Oxford, 1973), p. 16.

[7] Quoted in Calvin de Vries, "Peter De Vries: The Vale of Laughter" in *Theology Today,* Vol. XXXII, No. 1, p. 16.

[8] Cf. James Mackey, *The Problems of Religious Faith* (Chicago: Franciscan Herald Press, 1972), pp. 11-59.

[9] Howard Root, *Soundings* (Cambridge, 1962), p. 18.

[10] Annie Dillard, *Pilgrim at Tinker Creek* (New York: Bantam Books, Inc., 1975), pp. 1-2.

[11] Annie Dillard, *Holy The Firm* (New York: Harper & Row, Publishers, 1977), p. 67.

[12] The literature on the types of experiences people take as indications of a basic graciousness is vast. One of the most

Notes

readable is Peter Berger, *A Rumor of Angels* (New York: Doubleday, 1969). One of the most wide ranging is S. Paul Schilling, *God Incognito* (Nashville: Abingdon Press, 1974).

[13] King, p. 70.

[14] Kurt Vonnegut, Jr., *Cat's Cradle* (New York: Dell Publishing, 1963), p. 13.

[15] Paul Tillich, *Dynamics of Faith* (New York: Harper & Brothers Publishers, 1957), p. 101.

[16] Miguel de Unamuno, *The Agony of Christianity* (New York: Frederick Ungar Publishing., 1960), pp. 76-77.

[17] Nathan Scott, Jr., *The Broken Center* (Yale University Press, 1966), p. 91.

[18] Woody Allen. Quoted in Robert McAfee Brown, *Is Faith Obsolete? (Philadelphia: The Westminster Press, 1974)*, p. 86.

[19] In Peter De Vries' *Into Your Tent I'll Creep* (Boston: Little, Brown, 1971).

[20] Nikos Kazantzakis, *The Odyssey, A Modern Sequel* (New York: Simon and Schuster, 1958), p. 689.

[21] Joseph Dabney Bettis, ed., *Phenomenology of Religion* (New York: Harper & Row Publishers, 1969), p. 203.

[22] Kazantzakis, p. xxiii.

[23] Nikos Kazantzakis, *Zorba The Greek* (New York: Simon and Schuster, 1952), pp. 47-48.

[24] This act is dangerous because it can go wrong in at least two major ways. First, we can give ourselves to a false god. Our lives will be focused by this act but the focus will not be salvific. This is the classic move of idolatry, investing the drive for God in something other than God. Secondly, we can hand ourselves over to the true God but not receive ourselves back. This usually means we abdicate our responsibility to incarnate the values of God in the world. We will let God worry about his creation and we presume he will act even if we do not.

[25] Ian Ramsey, *Models and Mystery* (London: Oxford University Press, 1964), p. 17.

[26] Jon Sobrino, *Christology at the Crossroads* (Marynoll, New York: Orbis Books, 1978), p. 94.

[27] Ibid., 87.

John Shea

Chapter Three

[1] Edith Sitwell, The Collected Poems of Edith Sitwell (New York: The Vanguard Press, 1954), p. 302.

[2] Confer Philip J. Murnion, "The Parish as Source of Community and Identity" in The Parish in Community and Ministry (New York: Paulist Press, 1978), pp. 101-118.

[3] T. S. Eliot, "Tradition and the Individual Talent," in Modern Poets on Modern Poetry (Fontana Books, 1966), p. 61.

[4] John Macquarrie, Principles of Christian Theology (New York: Charles Scribner's Sons, 1966) pp. 92-93.

[5] Quoted in John Dominic Crossan, The Dark Interval (Niles, Illinois: Argus Communications, 1975), p. 19.

[6] Quoted in Amos N. Wilder, The New Voice (New York: Herder and Herder, 1969), p. 74.

[7] Amos Wilder, Early Christian Rhetoric: The Language of the Gospel (New York: Harper & Row, 1964), p. 84.

[9] Cf. John Haught, Religion and Self-Acceptance (New York: Paulist Press, 1976), pp. 148-52.

[8] Stephan Crites, "The Narrative Quality of Experience," Journal of the American Academy of Religion, Vol. XXXIX, 1971.

[10] Sam Keen, To A Dancing God (New York: Harper & Row, 1970), p. 86.

[11] Ibid., 103.

[12] Charles Winquest, "The Act of Storytelling and the Self's Homecoming," Journal of the American Academy of Religion, Vol., 42, 1974.

[13] Robert McAfee Brown, "My Story and 'The Story'" Theology Today, July, 1975.

[14] William A. Luijpen, Myth and Metaphysics (The Hague: Martinus Nijhoff, 1976), p. 111.

[15] Quoted in Annie Dillard, Pilgrim at Tinker Creek (New York: Bantam Books, Inc., 1975), pp. 30-31.

[16] Cf. Ian Ramsey, Talking about God," in Words About God (New York: Harper & Row, 1971), pp. 202-23.

[17] Annie Dillard, Holy The Firm (New York: Harper & Row, 1977), p. 47.

Notes

[18] John Shea, *The God Who Fell From Heaven* (Niles, Illinois: Argus Communications, 1979).

[19] Anne Sexton, *The Awful Rowing Toward God* (Boston: Houghton Mifflin Company, 1975), pp. 58-59.

[20] Nikos Kazantzakis, *Zorba the Greek* (New York: Simon and Schuster, 1952), p. 279.

[21] Leonardo Boff, *Jesus Christ Liberator* (Marynoll, New York: Orbis Books, 1978), p. 35.

[22] Robert Tannehill, *The Sword of His Mouth* (Philadelphia: Fortress Press, 1975), pp. 75-76.

[23] David Tracy, "The Catholic Analogical Imagination" in *Catholic Theological Society of America*, Proceedings of the Thirty-Second Annual Convention, Vol. 32, p. 242.

[24] Consult James Wm. McClendon, Jr., *Biography as Theology* (Nashville: Abingdon Press, 1974.) It is interesting to note that the Catholic culture of the immediate past relied heavily on the lives of the saints. Unfortunately, these life stories were often told in a maudlin and unconvincing fashion. Perhaps if the distinction between history and myth which is standard in biblical circles was applied to the lives of the saints, we might be able to recapture the power of their stories.

Chapter Four

[1] Nikos Kazantzakis, *The Last Temptation of Christ* (New York: Bantam Books, 1961), p. 2.

[2] Hermann Hesse, *Demian* (New York: Bantam Books, 1966), p. 4.

[3] D. Columba Marmion, *Christ the Life of the Soul* (St. Louis: B. Herder Book Co., 1928), p. 16.

[4] Quoted in James Wm. McClendon, Jr., *Biography as Theology* (Nashville: Abingdon Press, 1974), pp. 127-28.

[5] Cf. James P. Mackey, *Jesus, the Man and the Myth* (New York: Paulist Press, 1979), pp. 159-71.

[6] Leonardo Boff, *Jesus Christ Liberator* (Maryknoll, New York: Orbis Books, 1978), p. 77.

[7] John Cobb, Jr., "A Whiteheadean Christology" in *Process Philosophy and Christian Thought* (Indianapolis: The Bobbs-Merrill Company, Inc., 1971), p. 393.

[8] Mackey, p. 230.

[9] Jon Sobrino, *Christology at the Crossroads* (Maryknoll, New York: Orbis Books, 1978), p. 302.

[10] Reginald H. Fuller, *The Foundations of New Testament Christology* (New York: Charles Scribner's Sons, 1965), pp. 243-57.

[11] Mackey, p. 110.

[12] Ibid., 111.

[13] John Bowker, *The Religious Imagination and the Sense of God* (Oxford: Clarendon Press, 1978), pp. 121-138.

[14] Norman Perrin, *The New Testament: An Introduction* (New York: Harcourt Brace Jovanovich, Inc., 1974), pp. 287-88.

[15] Dermot Lane, *The Reality of Jesus* (New York: Paulist Press, 1975), p. 155.

[16] Hans Kung, *On Being A Christian* (New York: Doubleday & Co., 1976), p. 189.

[17] Ibid., 268.

[18] Edward Schillebeeckx, *Jesus* (New York: The Seabury Press, 1979), p. 302.

[19] Mary Gordon, *Final Payments* (New York: Ballantine Books, 1978), pp. 298-99.

[20] Kung, p. 179.

[21] William Faulkner, *Absalom, Absalom!* (New York: Random House, 1964), p. 251.